Illegal Immigration

OPPOSING
VIEWPOINTS®

Other Books of Related Interest

Illegal Immigration
OPPOSING VIEWPOINTS®

David Bender & Bruno Leone, *Series Editors*

Charles P. Cozic, *Book Editor*

OPPOSING
VIEWPOINTS®
SERIES

Greenhaven Press, Inc., San Diego, CA

Photo credit: Gazelle Technologies/Hulton Deutsch

Greenhaven Press, Inc.
PO Box 289009
San Diego, CA 92198-9009

Library of Congress Cataloging-in-Publication Data

Illegal immigration : opposing viewpoints / Charles P. Cozic, book editor.
    p.   cm. — (Opposing viewpoints series)
    Includes bibliographical references and index.
    ISBN 1-56510-514-1 (lib. bdg. : alk. paper). —
ISBN 1-56510-513-3 (pbk. : alk. paper)
    1. Illegal aliens—United States. 2. Emigration and immi-
gration law—United States. I. Cozic, Charles P., 1957–
II. Series: Opposing viewpoints series (Unnumbered)
KF4800.Z9I43   1997

                           96-22686
                             CIP

"Congress shall make no law . . .
abridging the freedom of speech,
or of the press."

First Amendment to the U.S. Constitution

The basic foundation of our democracy is the First Amendment
guarantee of freedom of expression. The Opposing Viewpoints
Series is dedicated to the concept of this basic freedom and the
idea that it is more important to practice it than to enshrine it.

Contents

Why Consider Opposing Viewpoints?

"The only way in which a human being can make some approach to knowing the whole of a subject is by hearing what can be said about it by persons of every variety of opinion and studying all modes in which it can be looked at by every character of mind. No wise man ever acquired his wisdom in any mode but this."

John Stuart Mill

In our media-intensive culture it is not difficult to find differing opinions. Thousands of newspapers and magazines and dozens of radio and television talk shows resound with differing points of view. The difficulty lies in deciding which opinion to agree with and which "experts" seem the most credible. The more inundated we become with differing opinions and claims, the more essential it is to hone critical reading and thinking skills to evaluate these ideas. Opposing Viewpoints books address this problem directly by presenting stimulating debates that can be used to enhance and teach these skills. The varied opinions contained in each book examine many different aspects of a single issue. While examining these conveniently edited opposing views, readers can develop critical thinking skills such as the ability to compare and contrast authors' credibility, facts, argumentation styles, use of persuasive techniques, and other stylistic tools. In short, the Opposing Viewpoints Series is an ideal way to attain the higher-level thinking and reading skills so essential in a culture of diverse and contradictory opinions.

In addition to providing a tool for critical thinking, Opposing Viewpoints books challenge readers to question their own strongly held opinions and assumptions. Most people form their opinions on the basis of upbringing, peer pressure, and personal, cultural, or professional bias. By reading carefully balanced opposing views, readers must directly confront new ideas as well as the opinions of those with whom they disagree. This is not to simplistically argue that everyone who reads opposing views will—or should—change his or her opinion. Instead, the series enhances readers' depth of understanding of their own views by encouraging confrontation with opposing ideas. Careful examination of others' views can lead to the readers' understanding of the logical inconsistencies in their own opinions, perspective on why they hold an opinion, and the consideration of the possibility that their opinion requires further evaluation.

Evaluating Other Opinions

To ensure that this type of examination occurs, Opposing Viewpoints books present all types of opinions. Prominent spokespeople on different sides of each issue as well as well-known professionals from many disciplines challenge the reader. An additional goal of the series is to provide a forum for other, less known, or even unpopular viewpoints. The opinion of an ordinary person who has had to make the decision to cut off life support from a terminally ill relative, for example, may be just as valuable and provide just as much insight as a medical ethicist's professional opinion. The editors have two additional purposes in including these less known views. One, the editors encourage readers to respect others' opinions—even when not enhanced by professional credibility. It is only by reading or listening to and objectively evaluating others' ideas that one can determine whether they are worthy of consideration. Two, the inclusion of such viewpoints encourages the important critical thinking skill of objectively evaluating an author's credentials and bias. This evaluation will illuminate an author's reasons for taking a particular stance on an issue and will aid in readers' evaluation of the author's ideas.

As series editors of the Opposing Viewpoints Series, it is our hope that these books will give readers a deeper understanding of the issues debated and an appreciation of the complexity of even seemingly simple issues when good and honest people disagree. This awareness is particularly important in a democratic society such as ours in which people enter into public debate to determine the common good. Those with whom one disagrees should not be regarded as enemies but rather as people whose views deserve careful examination and may shed light on one's own.

Thomas Jefferson once said that "difference of opinion leads to inquiry, and inquiry to truth." Jefferson, a broadly educated man, argued that "if a nation expects to be ignorant and free . . . it expects what never was and never will be." As individuals and as a nation, it is imperative that we consider the opinions of others and examine them with skill and discernment. The Opposing Viewpoints Series is intended to help readers achieve this goal.

David L. Bender & Bruno Leone,
Series Editors

Introduction

"Spending on illegal immigrants is out of control."

Michael Huffington, 1994

"There is little evidence showing that illegals are abusing social services."

Charles Mahtesian, Governing, May 1994

In 1992, police and welfare-fraud investigators in Walla Walla, Washington, uncovered an extensive illegal-document operation in the home of Celina Romero and two other illegal immigrants. Authorities contend that the immigrants were utilizing blank Social Security cards and counterfeit driver's licenses, U.S. passports, and birth certificates to draw an array of benefits.

At the time of her arrest, Romero was reportedly in the process of using a false surname to defraud the Internal Revenue Service of an $1,800 refund. According to experts, the making and selling of false documents for illegal immigrants is a thriving activity, particularly in larger cities.

However, immigrants and others assert that the goal of most illegal immigrants is not to commit fraud but simply to work hard to support their families. In the words of one illegal Guatemalan immigrant named Manuel, "I have no money, my family is hungry. All I'm doing is making life possible." Roberto Arellano, a former illegal immigrant, adds, "There is still much more opportunity for advancement here than in Mexico, and it is still possible to build a better life here."

Such contrary depictions of the aspirations and actions of illegal immigrants sustain the debate over illegal immigration. According to the Immigration and Naturalization Service, approximately 300,000 illegal immigrants enter the United States annually. Fearing what they perceive to be a growing problem, many Americans argue that government should adopt measures to make it less attractive for illegal immigrants to migrate to or remain in the country. Others, however, while agreeing it is necessary to discourage illegal immigrants from entering America, contend that government should not punish those illegal immigrants already residing in the United States.

Critics of illegal immigration, including many Democratic and

Republican politicians such as President Bill Clinton and conservative commentator Pat Buchanan, charge that illegal immigrants are drawn to the United States by the knowledge that they can receive free government benefits. According to federal law, illegal immigrants are entitled to receive public education, emergency health care under the Medicaid program, and, in some states, nutritional assistance for pregnant women. Their U.S.-born children, who automatically become citizens at birth, are eligible for a wide variety of benefits, including welfare payments.

According to writer George Sunderland, "Droves of illegals routinely enter California in order to obtain that state's high level of welfare payments. Services to illegal aliens now constitute almost 25 percent of California's social services budget." *Reader's Digest* writer Randy Fitzgerald contends that both poor and well-off undocumented immigrants enter the United States seeking benefits. Fitzgerald notes that in addition to impoverished pregnant immigrants who enter the United States illegally to bear children, thus gaining related benefits, even "wealthy foreign visitors take advantage of Medicaid loopholes to qualify for free care," including lifesaving surgery.

Hispanic and immigrants' rights activists respond that the vast majority of immigrants who cross the 2,000-mile U.S.-Mexico border illegally (an estimated 50 percent of whom are Mexican nationals) do so to escape poverty or repression in their native countries. These advocates argue that illegal immigrants believe America offers the best opportunities for them to better their lives. Many observers maintain that the high demand for cheap labor—rather than the prospect of social services—most attracts foreigners willing to enter illegally. According to Carlsbad, California, city official Jim Lundgren, "If [employers] weren't picking them up every day, they wouldn't be here."

Activists and others assert that illegal immigrants do not migrate to America to obtain public benefits and services. Urban Institute analysts Michael Fix and Jeffrey S. Passel contend that "welfare use among illegal immigrants is so low as to be undetectable, primarily because they are barred from virtually all benefit programs." For example, illegal immigrants are ineligible for Aid to Families with Dependent Children, food stamps, and housing and utilities assistance.

Many opponents of illegal immigration contend that laws are necessary to withhold the free benefits and services that attract undocumented residents. In 1994, California voters approved Proposition 187, which denied public education, health care, and welfare benefits to illegal immigrants and their U.S.-born children. (These provisions were immediately suspended pending judicial review.) In 1996, Congress passed similar immigration-reform bills that would disallow some of these benefits. According to Proposition 187 campaign leader Ron Prince, "What we are trying to do is encourage all illegal aliens to leave. We will do that by depriving them of public services. We will take away their jobs. We will take away their benefits."

But immigrants' rights activists and others maintain that such restrictive measures would deprive illegal immigrants of essential services, incite anti-immigrant sentiment, and do little to keep undocumented immigrants from crossing the border. Former U.S. education secretary William Bennett commented prior to Proposition 187's passage, "It is going to label all immigrants; it is going to turn into a war of colors, a war of races. It is poison in a democracy." Others argue that since illegal immigrants pay various taxes, they deserve to receive some services.

The advantages of living in the United States have traditionally attracted immigrants from around the world. But most Americans agree that the nation cannot accommodate all would-be immigrants. *Illegal Immigration: Opposing Viewpoints* examines what factors lure illegal immigrants to the United States and what measures would deter them. These issues are examined in the following chapters: Would New Measures Targeting Illegal Immigrants Be Fair? Do Illegal Immigrants Harm America? How Should America Respond to Illegal Immigration? Are Illegal Immigrants Being Victimized? The contributors in this anthology address these questions as they consider the presence of illegal immigrants in America.

Would New Measures Targeting Illegal Immigrants Be Fair?

Chapter Preface

In September 1994, California voters approved Proposition 187, legislation that bars illegal immigrants and their children from receiving certain public services such as education, health care, and welfare. (Portions of the measure were suspended in 1994 pending judicial review.) In 1996, both the U.S. Senate and House of Representatives passed restrictive bills (the Senate bill lacks a provision banning public education) that would remove federal mandates requiring states to provide benefits to illegal immigrants. Capitalizing on the popularity of these measures, activists in Arizona, Florida, and other states prepared similar initiatives for the ballot in 1996.

Proponents of such measures contend that providing illegal immigrants with public services drains billions of dollars from state budgets. According to California governor Pete Wilson, "[Federally] mandated services to illegal immigrants and their children are costing California taxpayers nearly $3 billion a year." Wilson and others object to illegal immigrants who enter the United States with the knowledge that they can easily receive free health care or other taxpayer-funded benefits.

However, others argue that since illegal immigrants pay a substantial amount of taxes, they should be entitled to essential services such as education and health care. According to Cecilia Munoz, a researcher for the National Council of La Raza, "These immigrants were already ineligible for welfare. The services to be cut, such as education, immunization, and prenatal care, are in the interest of the entire community." In Munoz's opinion, it would cost society less to provide basic benefits than to withhold them and risk creating an underclass of immigrants who are uneducated, unskilled, and in poor health.

Advocates of denying benefits to illegal immigrants maintain that dwindling public resources should be available only to deserving legal residents. Opponents respond that undocumented residents avoid using social services, relying on them only as a last resort. The authors in this chapter debate whether the new measures aimed at illegal immigrants are fair.

> *"An identity card [can] screen out illegal immigrants from the labor pool and government benefit programs."*

A Legal-Resident Identification System Would Be Fair

Joseph Nalven and Harry Bernstein

In Part I of the following two-part viewpoint, Joseph Nalven proposes two new identity cards—one for employment and the other for government benefits—that could effectively screen out illegal immigrants without violating individuals' civil liberties. In Part II, Harry Bernstein contends that the U.S. government should require job applicants to use a counterfeit-proof Social Security card to prove their legal status. Nalven is an anthropologist and a lawyer who has conducted research on illegal immigrants for the county of San Diego and the U.S. Department of Labor. Bernstein is a former labor writer for the *Los Angeles Times*.

As you read, consider the following questions:

1. Why do civil libertarians oppose a national identification card, according to Nalven?
2. According to Nalven, what techniques could make identification cards more reliable?
3. In Bernstein's opinion, when would the new Social Security card be used?

I

Any new law designed to curb the presence of illegal immigrants in the U.S. job market or from receiving entitlements will be lost or won in the details. The most important detail is an identity card to screen out illegal immigrants from the labor pool and government benefit programs.

We are accustomed to identifying ourselves with numbers—on driver licenses, Social Security cards, passports and health insurance programs as well as bank, gas station and store credit cards, even when enrolling in some book clubs. A few more cards would be tolerated, even welcomed, if the objective were to prevent illegal immigrants from using fraudulent identification or otherwise slipping into the job market or government benefit programs.

That was, in fact, the purpose proposed for using a national ID card prior to the passage of the Immigration Reform and Control Act of 1986. Civil libertarians helped defeat this proposal based on the belief that we would lose our freedom and privacy.

Digitized Identities

Times have changed. We have become accustomed to magnetic strips on the back of state driver licenses that contain personal histories. Credit cards often have holograms and photographs. Our names and personal characteristics have become the prize possession of junk mailers. The fight to maintain a secret self is losing ground to a digitized personality inside the electronic beehive.

The argument of civil libertarians has been made irrelevant by the proliferation of alphanumerical identifiers. The fear of a single system controlled by Big Brother is minimized by multiple identifiers, each tailored to a specific purpose. These are our cards of identity.

Thus, we can now return to the original objective of screening illegal immigrants out of the job market and from government benefits. Only two new cards of identity are needed—an employment ID card and one for government benefits. Should the civil libertarians insist, we can always carry more.

Commitment to Action

I would venture a guess that the majority of Americans are willing to carry more cards of identity to invigorate the process of screening illegal immigrants out of the job and benefit systems. The majority of Americans are overwhelmed by the continuing flow of illegal immigrants to the United States. Whether intended or not, the study by the Urban Institute (placing the cost of illegal immigration to California at $1.8 billion) will fuel the public's commitment to move beyond cost and benefit arguments to an action program. The Urban Institute's study misses the public understanding: Illegal immigrants have no equity stake in America unless we open the border, and there is not much support for that.

A Proper Strategy

We should concede this, namely that in totalitarian societies an ID is absolutely essential. The contrapositive, however, is not justified—that every society that has an ID will become a totalitarian society. As noted, already there is an ID of sorts, done by. Social Security. As a weapon against illegal immigration it is not reliable because it is very easy to get a Social Security card. But if a) it is a legitimate goal to regulate immigration, then b) the means to do this effectively should be there, and c) it would not appear to make sense to deny the government instruments that are not inherently cruel or indecent. To authorize an ID that merely proves you are who you say you are is not the same thing as to authorize a government enema or truth serum.

William F. Buckley Jr., *National Review*, August 28, 1995.

Current methods of identifying lawful presence in this country are, of course, cumbersome and encourage fraud and discrimination. Employers are expected to be junior immigration agents. They are not trained to weed out fraudulent documents. There is a temptation to second-guess the legitimacy of potential employee documents or to ignore documents altogether if the person appears to be a legal resident.

Even California's Employment Development Department abandoned pre-screening job applicants for employers. Not only did department workers complain of added work, but the procedure encouraged racial bitterness. One employee filed a declaration in support of an injunction to stop the EDD's screening process:

"One of my co-workers was threatened by an applicant who became extremely upset when told he could not be sent to a job referral because he did not have the proper identification."

Less Resentment and Fraud

If all citizens and legal residents had a uniform ID card, one for employment and another for government benefits, we could expect less resentment and less discrimination. We could also expect less fraud, given the improved technology of making cheap and near tamper-proof cards (for example by fingerprinting, or putting in holograms or photos).

Without an effective screening mechanism, there is more

abuse of regulated systems and markets, both for illegal immigrants and citizens. Entitlement and employment cards of identity can significantly reduce illegal immigrants' abuse of government services and the labor market. They also will circumvent the concerns of civil libertarians by being limited to specific uses. And they will minimize discrimination and ethnic resentment that arise from the present identification system.

II

Maybe linking a compassionate liberal idea to a tough new law-enforcement proposal would get even a conservative Congress to adopt a plan that could quell the emotional turmoil created by Proposition 187 [a 1994 measure approved by California voters that prohibits illegal immigrants from receiving most public benefits] and help resolve the problems of illegal immigration.

The Immigration Reform and Control Act of 1986 gave amnesty to illegal immigrants who had lived here continuously before 1982, but it wrongly ignored the mass of more recently arrived immigrants.

For the first time, the law set penalties for employers who knowingly hire illegal immigrants as a way of getting an inexpensive and compliant labor force. The law has failed, however, because employer penalties were almost entirely unenforced.

Congress must dare to pass an even more generous amnesty law for illegal immigrants already here. It would be opposed by many who backed Proposition 187 because it would nullify the effect of the measure on illegal immigrants now in this country and do it without a lengthy, costly court battle. But to reduce that inevitable opposition and avoid the need for future amnesty laws, Congress must also pass and the Administration must stringently enforce much tougher laws containing severe penalties against employers who hire illegal immigrants to take advantage of their cheap labor.

A New Social Security Card

A new amnesty law must require every job applicant to produce a counterfeit-resistant Social Security card, similar to one recommended by a bipartisan, blue-ribbon federal commission on immigration reform. Let's make the new card at least as secure as credit cards. The law should clearly state that the new card would not be a national identification card that workers must carry at all times, but an identification used only to verify legal applicants for jobs, the main attraction for undocumented immigrants.

Since everyone would have to have the card, discrimination based on skin color should not be a problem. If there was any, it could be remedied by existing anti-discrimination laws.

A counterfeit-proof Social Security card would be similar to computerized systems that guarantee the validity of millions of credit cards in circulation—cards that are secure enough to allow the companies distributing them to make billions with relatively little fraudulent use.

At first, the 1986 immigration measure appeared to slow the flow of illegal workers—apprehensions, which had reached a high of 1.8 million in 1986, fell below 1 million in 1989. But when it became clear that there would be little or no enforcement of the law, the number of apprehensions grew sharply in 1990 and have climbed steadily since; 1.3 million aliens were apprehended in 1993. Profit-hungry employers were delighted, as were job-hungry illegal immigrants. There was no adequate way for honest employers to readily and accurately identify those here legally.

The First Amnesty Law

The first amnesty allowed more than 1 million illegal immigrants the right to stay and work on U.S. farms. Nationally, another 4 million undocumented workers were granted amnesty to work in any industry. No other country has ever adopted such a generous amnesty law.

Some contend that legal residents just won't do the hard, dirty jobs that illegal immigrants are willing to perform. The truth is that citizens and other legal residents elsewhere in this country do the very same jobs done by illegal immigrants in a few states like California. And there are few real labor shortages.

While there are extremists who want an open border, allowing anyone who wants to come here to do so legally, polls show that most opponents of Proposition 187 say that something should be done about illegal immigration.

On the other side, few supporters of the measure can seriously expect that those here illegally will leave voluntarily just because they can't get government services. Nor would they expect any general support for rounding up millions of those now here illegally and shipping them back to their countries of origin—an ugly and impossible task.

Thus if we make almost certain that jobs will not be open to future illegal immigrants by requiring counterfeit-proof Social Security cards, denying them most free government benefits and services (but not emergency medical care), while at the same time stepping up patrol of the border (but not building a wall between our country and Mexico), the United States could finally gain control over its borders, welcome legal immigrants and end the severe competition for jobs that citizens and others here legally must face from the illegal workers.

"You might just want to call [a national identification card] a passport to hell, because for a lot of us, that's what it will be."

A Legal-Resident Identification System Would Be Unfair

Glenn Garvin

A nationwide system of identifying legal residents for employment purposes would be prone to much error and fraud and would be unfair to Americans, Glenn Garvin argues in the following viewpoint. Garvin maintains that unreliable techniques such as an identification card or telephone verification system, combined with the Immigration and Naturalization Service's (INS) faulty databases, would be exploited by illegal aliens and would jeopardize immigrants' and native-born Americans' right to work. Garvin is a contributing editor for *Reason*, a monthly libertarian magazine.

As you read, consider the following questions:

1. What are "feeder documents," according to Garvin?
2. According to Peter Larrabee, cited by Garvin, how often does the INS incorrectly verify work eligibility?
3. According to the author, how long did it take the INS to hand-search job applicants' files in 1992?

Excerpted from "Bringing the Border War Home" by Glenn Garvin. Reprinted, with permission, from the October 1994 issue of *Reason* magazine. Copyright 1995 by the Reason Foundation, 3415 S. Sepulveda Blvd., Suite 400, Los Angeles, CA 90034.

About 20 people work in [Los Angeles accountant] Ruben Jauregui's office, which he calls "a little United Nations." His staff includes natives of China, Taiwan, Hong Kong, India, South Korea, Switzerland, Venezuela, Mexico, and Chile. Each one of them is required to fill out an INS [Immigration and Naturalization Service] I-9 form, attesting to his eligibility to work in the United States. Then each one has to show Jauregui a document to verify that eligibility.

"There are about 30 *types* of documents they can use to satisfy the I-9, and then there are subsets of those types that include dozens and dozens of other documents," Jauregui notes. "I'm not going to sit here and tell you that we have a litmus test for each one, that we can authenticate each one. There's no way."

Hundreds of Documents

Indeed, an employer not only has to be able to tell the difference between all kinds of arcane INS permits, from the I-94 form to the I-551 stamp, but among literally hundreds of documents generated by other state, local, and federal authorities. Do you know what a Kentucky driver's license is supposed to look like? How about a South Dakota voter registration card? A Hopi Indian tribal document? A U.S. Coast Guard merchant mariner card? A Virgin Islands birth certificate? A Tucumcari, New Mexico, school district ID card? A patient record from the Norton Sound Health Corporation hospital in Nome, Alaska? All those and many, many more are on the list of documents that employers must accept.

"It is just overwhelming for many employers to have to inspect these documents," says Matthew Bartosiak, a senior consultant with the Employers Group, a nonprofit association that assists California companies with personnel issues.

> You almost have to be an immigration attorney to have a full understanding of all these documents. You have people walking in every day, all day long, with different documents with different expiration dates and different conditions attached to them. They are seemingly endless. The INS issues a booklet with samples of some—but it's far from all of them. And the booklet is printed in black and white, which is not very helpful when you're dealing with color documents.
>
> Employers are required by law not to knowingly hire people with fraudulent documents. And on the other hand they have to be careful not to discriminate against anyone, or they're vulnerable to a lawsuit. . . . They're told, Be particular, but not too particular—don't discriminate. It's a very thin line employers are always walking, a very tough line. And employers are not documentation specialists. . . .

Why can't an employer just call the INS and ask if an immigrant is eligible to work? In these days of computerized data-bases, that shouldn't be so hard to rig up.

That very thought has occurred, more than once, in Washington. In 1992, the INS conducted an experiment with telephone verification at nine companies scattered around the country, ranging from the little Modern Italian Bakery in Oakdale, New York, to the giant Houston-based construction firm Brown and Root.

Each company paid $775 for what the INS called a "point-of-sale device," a little computerized gizmo that attaches to a telephone, closely resembling the thing merchants use to verify credit card numbers. Anytime an immigrant applied for a job at any of the nine companies, his name, birth date, and alien registration number were punched into the device, which relayed them to an INS computer in Washington. In a moment, the computer popped back with a message authorizing employment.

That was the theory, anyway. The reality was that 28 percent of the time, the INS computer could find no record of the immigrant and ordered the employer to send in the name on paperwork so that a clerk could search the records by hand—a process that took up to two weeks for each request. Two-thirds of those cyberspasms turned out to be caused by keypunch errors or missing INS files, not immigrants sneaking into the country without INS approval. Ultimately, only about 9 percent of the immigrants were ruled ineligible to work. That means there were 19 percent who *were* eligible but who had to wait, along with their employers, while INS clerks rummaged through their files.

An 81 percent success rate is pretty good if you're shooting basketball free throws. It's abysmally low when you're playing with people's lives. (And the error rate doesn't even count the caprices of the INS computer. One day, for instance, it simply refused to consider any first name beginning with the letter Z.) But the Bill Clinton administration was so delighted with the telephone verification program that it is expanding it to 1,000 companies.

A Colossal Loophole

What's truly amazing about this is that, quite aside from the high error rate, the telephone verification system has a colossal loophole that makes it utterly useless: It depends on a job applicant confessing that he's a resident alien. All an illegal immigrant has to do is lie and say he's an American citizen; then his name is never submitted to the computer.

Well, then, why not link the INS computers with the Social Security Administration's and verify *everybody's* name, regardless of citizenship? It still won't work. "What if I walk in and give my mother's Social Security number, or a friend's, or one I buy from somebody on the street?" asks Cecilia Muñoz, senior immigration policy analyst of the National Council of La Raza, a

Latino lobbying group. "You can't just have a phone-in system without some way to prove a person's identification. And the way to do that is with a card."

A card. It sounds so benign. You might call it, as California Sen. Dianne Feinstein does, a "machine-readable card that all job and benefits applicants would be required to present to verify their work or eligibility for assistance." Or you could call it a national ID card and work permit, because that's what it is. Or you might just want to call it a passport to hell, because for a lot of us, that's what it will be. At the very least it will put every American's right to earn a living at the mercy of the federal government's whimsical computers. And at the very worst—which, history teaches us, we have every right to expect—it will be a brutally effective tool for the surveillance, manipulation, and punishment of anyone who runs afoul of Washington's imperious corps of social engineers.

Feinstein's Card

Nearly all the anti-immigration warriors, from Peter Brimelow [author of *Alien Nation*] to Rep. Barney Frank, favor a national ID card. There are various proposals for the form a card might take, but the most chic around Washington is the one proposed by Feinstein.

Feinstein's ID would look very similar to a credit card, with a strip of magnetic tape across the back. Encoded on the tape, along with your Social Security number, is your thumbprint. A potential employer inserts your card in a computerized reader, then asks you to put your thumb on an optical scanner. The computer compares your thumb to the print on the card, and, if everything's kosher, it phones a Social Security/INS computer in Washington, which decides whether you're eligible for a job. The fingerprint stuff may sound a little science fictionish, but the scanning equipment is already being commercially marketed. (The *price*, though, may read like science fiction to many of the small businesses required to buy the scanner-readers: $2,000 apiece.)

Feinstein says this process will be "fraud-resistant" and "counterfeit-resistant." Perhaps this claim is best evaluated by a professional fraud and counterfeiter.

"There really is nothing you can make that's 100 percent tamper-proof or 100 percent fraud-proof," says Frank Abagnale. "That's one of the reasons I don't think there will ever be a national ID card. We don't even have very good money. It's the worst currency in the world, printed with technology that's 75 years old. It's pathetically easy to counterfeit. I don't see how the government can come out with a secure ID when it can't even come up with a good dollar bill."

25

Abagnale speaks with some authority on the subject of counterfeiting: A boy wonder of the world of bunko, he forged $2.5 million in checks by the time he was 25, passing phony paper in 26 different countries. Two decades ago, he went straight and began working as a secure-document consultant. He designed the American Express Official Check, the company's version of a cashier's check, and the Clinton administration consulted with him on its doomed national health card.

SAYS HERE THE NEW IMMIGRATION LAW IS VIOLATING THE RIGHTS OF MINORITIES...

INS

GAO REPORT

EMPLOYER SANCTIONS ARE CAUSING WIDESPREAD DISCRIMINATION AGAINST HISPANICS...

GAO

DISCRIMINATION? WE CAN'T HAVE THAT!

WE'LL HAVE TO VIOLATE EVERYONE'S RIGHTS!

NATIONAL WORKER I.D.

PASS CARD 123-456-789

© John Trever. Used with permission.

"In California, they spent a fortune on their new driver's licenses," the Tulsa-based Abagnale observes. "They put holograms in them, used sophisticated sealants in the printing, just poured money into the design. And a few months after it was introduced, they arrested a forger with 50 licenses in 50 different names. I told them, All you've done is stop some kid from changing the birthdate on his license in order to buy a beer."

Feeder Documents

The anecdote about the driver's license is telling, because it leads to the unlocked back door into the national ID card: the ease with which all the "feeder documents"—the documents from which any federal verification database will be drawn—can be forged.

"Look, I designed the state of Florida's birth certificate," says Abagnale.

It's got a street price in Miami of $5,000, so it's obviously a very valuable document. But it's still ridiculously easy to defeat all the security I put into it. I'll tell you how. A forger comes to Miami, goes to the Bureau of Vital Statistics and asks to see the death records for 1948. They'll let him view them in the office. He picks out an infant who died at birth and copies down all the information it's got there—the mother's name, the father's, the time of birth, all that stuff.

Then he walks right down the hall to another office where he can apply for a certified copy of the birth certificate. All he has to do to get it is to pay $5.00. And once he has that, he goes across town to a Motor Vehicle Department office and gets a driver's license in the name of the baby on the birth certificate. And with a driver's license, he can apply for all kinds of documents. For just 50 bucks, you can create 10 different identities for yourself in just a couple of days.

"I don't think people understand how many loopholes will be built into any attempt to create a national ID card," says immigration attorney Peter Larrabee.

It has to do with the way our government is structured, federal rights versus states' rights. We have no federal birth card. Every state registers births differently, and none of them has ever made security a high priority.

Birth certificates in Texas, for instance, were not even centrally registered until 1948. And even then it was done in a pretty slipshod way. Any birth reported to the state was just written in a big ledger book, without requiring any doctor's signature or anything.

Not that federal records are much more reliable. Until 1972, the Social Security Administration would take an applicant's word about his age and identity when issuing cards. In 1991, Gwendolyn King, the agency's commissioner, testified to Congress that more than 60 percent of Social Security numbers were based on unverified statements. "That, of course, means that the Social Security number simply cannot be used effectively as a means of identification," she added.

Red Tape and Errors

The only ones likely to find a national ID card a significant obstacle to working will be honest people who become accidentally snarled in red tape. And there are likely to be a lot of them. The card will depend heavily on INS records to establish work eligibility—records that, a 1989 Justice Department audit found, are incorrect 17 percent of the time. And a lot of people think that figure is way too low.

"The databases were not very good when I worked for the

INS, and they're worse now," says attorney Larrabee. "I'd say they're wrong 50 percent of the time, and that's being generous." In one recent case, Larrabee represented a San Diego sock factory where the INS claimed to have found 15 illegal aliens working. But it turned out that nine had legal work permits, and two weren't even aliens—they were U.S. citizens. "I've had several other clients who experience 50 percent or greater error at the hands of the INS," he adds.

Because the victims of INS screw-ups are typically foreigners at the bottom end of the economic food chain, we hear little about them. But that will certainly change when the national ID card comes on line. A GAO [General Accounting Office] study in 1988 showed that about 65 million people in the United States change jobs or enter the work force each year. Let's suppose that somehow the INS, through a superhuman effort that defies all our previous experience with federal bureaucracy, whittles its error rate down to a minuscule 1 percent. That's 650,000 people thrown out of work by mistake *every year*. The vast majority of them are bound to be U.S. citizens, native-born and bred.

Of course, they'll get their jobs back. Eventually. When the computer goofed during the 1992 test of the telephone verification system, it took the INS up to two weeks to search a job applicant's file by hand. And that was dealing with 2,668 searches over the course of a year. How long will the searches take when there are 650,000 a year? Six weeks? A month? Two months? And while the unlucky victim of the computer is waiting, who will pay his rent and buy his groceries? Perhaps the Feinsteins and Brimelows will show an unexpected humanitarian streak and permit workers bounced by the computer to start working while their cases are investigated. But that will force companies to invest weeks or months in training employees who may not even be eligible to work. . . .

"The really horrible thing about this is that what we're talking about here with the 650,000 is a *really optimistic* scenario—an unrealistically optimistic scenario," observes John Miller of the Center for Equal Opportunity, a pro-immigration think tank.

> Imagine a 5 percent scenario and you're up to 3.25 million people thrown out of work. Or a 10 percent scenario, with 6.5 million out of work. Either of those is probably more likely.

> The estimates of the illegal immigrant population of the United States run between 3 million and 4 million, out of a U.S. population of 260 million. That means maybe 1.5 percent of the U.S. population is illegal. Because of the actions of 1.5 percent of the population, suddenly the federal government has to monitor all the employment decisions made in this country? Doesn't that seem like a classic example of overreach?

"Proposition 187 may not dent illegal immigration, but it is emphatically not demonic."

Laws Denying Benefits to Illegal Immigrants Are Fair

Bruce Fein and Linda Seebach

In 1994, California voters approved Proposition 187, which aimed to deny public benefits such as education and health care to illegal immigrants. The proposition was immediately challenged by state and federal courts and the case was expected to eventually reach the Supreme Court. In Part I of the following two-part viewpoint, Bruce Fein argues that illegal immigrants are not entitled to public benefits and that the denial of benefits is not punitive or unjust. In Part II, Linda Seebach contends that fair play and respect for current laws demand that benefits should not be extended to illegal aliens. Fein is a Virginia attorney specializing in constitutional, international, and communications law. Seebach is an editorial writer for the *Los Angeles Daily News*.

As you read, consider the following questions:

1. In Fein's opinion, how should illegal immigrants obtain health care services?
2. According to Seebach, who would be responsible for verifying students' legal status?
3. What will be the outcome for illegal immigrants now in California schools, in Seebach's opinion?

OUACHITA TECHNICAL COLLEGE

I

Never in the annals of American jurisprudence have so many maligned a law for so little.

In November 1994, California voters approved Proposition 187, a so-called anti–illegal immigration measure. It was vituperated in a *Legal Times* column by Stuart Taylor Jr. as "barbaric," "cruel," and "Stalinist," although the Soviet Union was never besieged by illegal immigrants. Indeed, Taylor implies, the consummate ugliness of Proposition 187 should prompt the few remaining decent Americans (like himself) to consider trading democracy for something else—maybe rule by Platonic guardians.

But Taylor's flagellation of Proposition 187 proponents is evocative of an inimitable Churchillian quip regarding the chaste and censorious Sir Stafford Cripps: "[T]here, but for the grace of God, goes God."

Proposition 187 may not dent illegal immigration, but it is emphatically not demonic. It generously provides publicly funded emergency health care to illegal aliens, and merely continues their current ineligibility for welfare and other benefit programs. It does refuse subsidies for treatment of non-emergency ailments, and excludes illegals from public schooling. And it requires government officials to report persons suspected of illegal status to the Immigration and Naturalization Service [INS].

Legitimate Concerns

What is wrong-headed about denying welfare largesse to illegals? California is legitimately concerned with husbanding its scarce revenues for the benefit of those with demonstrated allegiance to the United States. Further, as the Supreme Court lectured in *Dandridge v. Williams*, 397 U.S. 471 (1970): "[T]he Constitution does not empower this Court to second guess state officials charged with the difficult responsibility of allocating limited public welfare funds among the myriad of potential recipients."

Excluding illegals from welfare benefits also at least marginally assists the national interest in staunching illegal immigration, which is a federal crime. And even for citizens, public welfare is no constitutional command.

Taylor insinuates that *sans* welfare, the starving bodies of illegal aliens will clutter the sidewalks. If that ghastly prospect were realistic, then Proposition 187 should be heralded as the illegal immigration panacea. Who would crave to enter the United States to die of starvation?

In any event, Taylor seems disbelieving of his own prophecy: He salutes the present laws' ban on "welfare, food stamps, and most other state and federal benefit programs" for illegal aliens.

Nor is the exclusion of illegals from free non-emergency health care unjust. The vast majority of illegal immigrants are employed and should pay for health services, not sponge off citizens. If demand for payment is thought to be too stern, illegals in need of medical services should return to their native lands, as mandated by federal immigration laws. The billions born outside the United States enjoy no moral entitlement to health-care subsidies here, based on their craftiness in evading criminal prohibitions on illegal entry.

Costing Taxpayers Billions

The federal government forces states to give health care, education and other benefits to individuals who are in our country illegally. These mandated services to illegal immigrants and their children are costing California taxpayers nearly $3 billion a year.

Saving just the $1 billion we spend educating illegal immigrants in California schools would allow us to put a new computer on every 5th grader's school desk; provide pre-school services to an additional 67,000 4-year-olds; expand Healthy Start Centers to an additional 750 sites; and provide 12.5 million tutorial and mentoring hours to at-risk youth.

Depriving legal California residents of these services is wrong. I'm urging Congress to repeal the federal mandates that require states to provide health care, education and other benefits to illegal immigrants.

Pete Wilson, *Spectrum*, Winter 1994.

The ineligibility of illegals for public schooling may be imprudent, but "barbaric" or "cruel" seem misplaced disparagements. If those terms were apt, the prospect of ineligibility would virtually end illegal immigration. Only a handful of stone-hearted parents would smuggle their children into the United States to be greeted by government viciousness. In any event, reserving public-schools slots for children enjoying legal status—and thus ordinarily destined to play a role in public life—seems far from irrational.

Plyler v. Doe

The Supreme Court's 5-4 ruling in *Plyler v. Doe*, 457 U.S. 202 (1982), voiding a Texas public-school exclusion of illegal aliens under the equal protection clause of the Fourteenth Amendment, seems ill-reasoned and ripe for overruling. The Court equated the exclusion with visiting the sins of parents guilty of immigration crimes on the heads of their illegal offspring: "Even if the State found it expedient to control the conduct of adults by acting against their children, legislation directing the onus of a parent's misconduct against this children does not comport with fundamental conceptions of justice."

But school exclusions for illegals are not punitive; they neither incarcerate, fine, nor stigmatize. They are vastly milder than deportation of illegal alien children—a fate that aroused no compunctions in the *Plyler* majority—although the child deportees are innocent of misconduct. Deportation, of course, deprives the children of any opportunity for an education in the United States, either public or private.

The *Plyler* majority found no evidence of congressional immigration policy sympathetic to public-school exclusions. But since that 1982 decision, Congress has toughened immigration laws, and has generally withheld federal welfare benefits from illegals. For example, it made criminal the knowing employment of illegal aliens in the Immigration Reform and Control Act of 1986. Congress has also denied illegal immigrants the right to food stamps, medical care, and aid to families with dependent children. Proposition 187 sits harmoniously within that orchestra of recent federal immigration laws.

The constitutional pivots of *Plyler* thus seem fragile, especially because only one of its thin five-member majority remains on the high court.

Parallel Duties

Taylor melodramatically apprehends a Stalinist police state in the aftermath of Proposition 187. But the reporting duties the proposition imposes on publicly funded health facilities to notify the INS of suspected illegal aliens are parallel to their obligations regarding suspected cases of child neglect or abuse. Federal law, for example, requires a broad spectrum of health-care and child-care providers—doctors, nurses, teachers, social workers, psychologists, and foster parents—to report reasonably suspected instances of neglect or abuse. Those obligations have not turned children into snitches on their parents.

Nor will the reporting requirements on school officials have that effect. (Proposition 187 also requires public-school authorities to confirm the legal status of enrollees and their parents, and report suspected cases of illegal status.) The initiative neither directs nor empowers school authorities to enlist children as informants against their parents in determining whether the latter are illegal aliens. That abuse might occur—and should be stopped if it does—but to calumniate Proposition 187 as a "Stalinist-snitch" law before implementation has begun is reminiscent of the Queen of Hearts in *Alice in Wonderland*: "Sentence first—verdict afterwards."

After flogging Proposition 187 proponents as senseless barbarians, Taylor betrays his genuine moral gripe: "[A]ll immigration restrictions are cruel. . . ." Since Taylor is against cruelty, unrestricted immigration would seem to be his moral imperative.

But Taylor's gripe against immigration restrictions and deterrents should be aimed at Congress. It is that institution that is endowed with the exclusive constitutional prerogative of relaxing or reforming immigration laws. To cannonade at Proposition 187, confined to those made illegal by Congress, is like Cleopatra's assault on the messenger for bringing bad news.

II

Editor's note: The following viewpoint was originally published one day before the passage of Proposition 187.

There's plenty to disapprove of in Proposition 187, and I'm going to vote for it anyway. It is essential for the people of California to declare without equivocation that they will no longer tolerate massive violation of U.S. law or public officials who wink at it.

I agree that there are less sweeping or constitutionally questionable measures that legislators could adopt to reduce the burdens of illegal immigration.

But I haven't seen any sign that our leaders in Washington or Sacramento plan to do that any time soon, and if California's voters reject 187, they will have the perfect excuse for continuing inaction: "See? It can't really be so bad as people were claiming. After all, 187 didn't pass."

Given the hysterical excesses of much anti-187 rhetoric, and the pro-187 campaign's difficulty in making itself heard, it's no wonder that polls show support is eroding. Opponents typically misrepresent what the measure says, claiming, for instance, that teachers will have to report students they suspect are in the country illegally.

That's not true. . . . Even in the rather unlikely event that the education provisions go into effect—which would require a Supreme Court decision and probably take years—it would be schools, not teachers, who would have the responsibility of verifying eligibility.

That's not different, in principle, from what they do now. If you're an American parent, you can't just show up and enroll your little darling in any school you fancy; you have to prove you're entitled, by residence, to have the child in that school in that district. Why is it immoral to require the same of people who are citizens of another country?

Cost Concerns

And if you're worried about the cost of litigation to overturn *Plyler v. Doe*, the Supreme Court decision that established the right of children to education even if they are illegally present in the country, you should worry even harder about the costs of not trying to overturn it.

It is powerfully corrupting to have large numbers of people whose own livelihood depends on the illegal activities of others. You saw that in the self-serving arguments advanced by people in the Los Angeles Unified Schools District, who said, in effect, that they were opposed to ending illegal immigration because they'd lose their jobs.

If that's a problem now, it's because the number of illegal aliens is so large. With no effective means to prevent illegal immigration, and no disposition even to discourage it, the number will simply grow larger and the costs more unsupportable.

Supporters of uncontrolled immigration say illegal aliens come not to receive benefits but to work. That's probably true, but once they are here, they do receive benefits—not least, birthright citizenship for their children born in America.

And as for working, pray tell at what? If people are present in the country illegally, it's also illegal for them to work and for anyone to hire them. If they come in order to work, that is, it is with the full intention of continuing to break the law, every single day of their lives here. And people who are working illegally are hardly in a position to pay their fair share of taxes.

Enforcing the employment law, if anyone seriously tried to do it, would be as threatening to legal residents as anything in 187. . . .

Respect for the Law

No one is going to remove or deport the hundreds of thousands of illegal aliens now in California schools, whatever happens to 187 or *Plyler v. Doe.* The urgent problem is to reduce the incoming flood to a trickle.

America does not need to sacrifice its freedoms to accomplish that. I've lived as a legal resident alien in two countries, Switzerland and China. Now China really is a police state. But believe me, the fact that as a visually identifiable racial minority I was constantly being required to prove my residence status came a long way down on my list of things to worry about.

In Switzerland, too, I often needed to show my visa—to buy a car, to rent a hotel room, to go to the hospital. And there was no way I could have held a job, which was contrary to the conditions of my visa, without running into officialdom.

Switzerland is not a police state; it has been a democracy for seven hundred years. It has succeeded in staying that way, in part, because the Swiss are a law-abiding people themselves and they require foreigners who want to live there to obey the law as well.

Respect for the law is necessary for the preservation of freedom.

"The War on Immigrants is being more openly coordinated and directed from the highest ranks of the central government."

Laws Denying Benefits to Illegal Immigrants Are Unfair

Revolutionary Worker

According to the *Revolutionary Worker* (*RW*) in the following viewpoint, California's Proposition 187 (which includes a provision that denies some public benefits to illegal immigrants) is one sign of the capitalist system's escalating "war" against illegal immigrants. The *RW* maintains that whether U.S. courts uphold or strike down the proposition, the federal government will increase its repressive treatment of legal and illegal immigrants. The *Revolutionary Worker* is a publication of the Revolutionary Communist Party.

As you read, consider the following questions:

1. In the *Revolutionary Worker's* opinion, what was one of the biggest myths promoted about Proposition 187?
2. How did people in Los Angeles protest Proposition 187, according to the *RW*?
3. According to the *RW*, what legal-immigrant benefits are targeted by immigration proposals?

Abridged from "Government Escalates War on Immigrants," *Revolutionary Worker*, January 14, 1996. Reprinted by permission of the *Revolutionary Worker*, the weekly newspaper of the Revolutionary Communist Party, U.S.A. Greenhaven editors have retitled and added some subheadings and a boxed quotation to the original article.

In November 1994 a vicious "ballot initiative" aimed against immigrants—known as Proposition 187—was voted into law in California. Shortly after the election a lawsuit filed by some opponents of Prop 187 put enforcement of the new law on hold. A year later—in late November 1995—U.S. District Judge Mariana Pfaelzer issued rulings on the suit. The judge upheld some parts of Prop 187. At the same time, she ruled that some other parts of 187 could not be applied as they were written, because they deal with areas of the law that only the federal government can control.

The people need to understand what this court decision is about—because it reveals some things about how the system intends to *intensify* its War on Immigrants. And learning more about what the ruling class is up to is an important part of building a more powerful resistance to the attacks coming down against our immigrant brothers and sisters.

What the Court Ruled

Prop 187 was based on and promoted the Big Lie—that immigrants who come to the United States don't contribute anything productive to U.S. society and therefore should not be allowed any of its "benefits." The main provisions of 187 aimed to: deny immigrants access to schools and hospitals; force teachers, doctors and administrators to become snitches by requiring them to report immigrants without official documents to the Immigration and Naturalization Service (INS or La Migra); give heavy penalties to anyone who makes or uses non-official IDs; and require the police to report the immigration status of everyone they arrest to La Migra, so that people without papers could be deported.

California Governor Pete Wilson got behind 187 big time. TV stations and major newspapers in California let loose with a media barrage that tried to make it seem as if just about everyone in the state was for clamping down on immigrants. One of the biggest myths promoted about Prop 187 was that it was a "grassroots initiative" which supposedly originated among ordinary people, rather than political representatives of the capitalist system. The fact is, 187 was designed and promoted from the beginning to push the extremely repressive anti-immigrant agenda of the capitalist ruling class. 187 has been used by boozhwah [bourgeois] politicians to justify intensifying and extending attacks on immigrants which were already well under way before it was passed. Leading up to the vote for 187, an intense campaign of TV spots, political ads and newspaper headlines stirred up a hate-filled atmosphere of hysteria and lies about immigrants among some sections of the population in California. As the *RW* wrote shortly after Prop 187 was passed, "The main purpose of Prop 187 was to turn this public opinion into a reactionary 'popular mandate' for an anti-immigrant program the government is already carrying out against the people. The dirty secret is that no matter what the outcome of the vote on 187, the system had plans for going after the immigrants."

A Split Ruling

The November 1995 ruling by the U.S. district court had two main aspects. Judge Pfaelzer upheld portions of Prop 187 entirely. She also ruled that some other sections could not stand as they were written, because the federal government has jurisdiction over these areas of law which 187 tried to turn into the responsibility of the state of California.

Pfaelzer's ruling said that "illegal immigrants" could be barred from health and social services that are funded entirely by California's state government. According to the *L.A. Times,* this consists "primarily of prenatal and long-term elderly care." In other words, the court ruled that California can begin cutting off pregnant women and older folks from state-funded health care. She also ruled that the section of 187 which calls for immigrants to be excluded from "public post-secondary educational institutions" (state universities and community colleges) can be enforced.

The court also ruled that the section of 187 which provides heavy state penalties for the "manufacture, distribution, or sale of false citizenship or resident documents" can stand as it is. Also left standing is the section which punishes the "use of false citizenship or resident documents" with penalties of five years and $25,000.

The judge noted that the section of 187 which sparked the most outrage and protest deals with areas of law that only the federal government can control. These are the sections that barred many immigrant children from schools and required school administrators to report to La Migra children they "suspected" of not having the correct papers; barred immigrants completely from publicly funded health care and required hospitals to report their patients to the immigration authorities; and required local police departments to verify the immigration status of everyone they arrested and notify La Migra of those they thought should be deported. Another section of 187 which required the attorney general of California, as well as the federal government, to keep records of all immigrants without papers was also ruled to be entering into the jurisdiction of the federal government.

Ruling Class Fear of Mass Opposition

Because Judge Pfaelzer ruled that several parts of 187 cannot be applied as they were written, some people opposed to 187 and to the attacks on immigrants are coming out with the mistaken summation that this is a ruling favorable to the people. A health care administrator who is against 187 said to the *L.A. Times*, "We're ecstatic about the ruling." One of the lawyers who had argued against 187 before Judge Pfaelzer said, "Proposition 187 effectively has been thrown out by the federal courts."

It is not really true that 187 has been "thrown out"—and it would be a big mistake for people opposed to 187 to let down their guard or to put their hopes in Pfaelzer's court, or any other court.

The judge herself stated the thinking at the heart of her ruling: "The California voters' overwhelming approval of Proposition 187 reflects their justifiable frustration with the federal government's inability to enforce the immigration laws effectively. No matter how serious the problem may be, however, the authority to regulate immigration belongs exclusively to the federal government."

The judge did not say that the essence of what Prop 187 seeks to implement is wrong, illegal or unconstitutional. Her main argument was that some parts of 187—such as kicking kids out of schools because their parents can't produce acceptable ID papers; denying health care to whole categories of people because of where they were born; deporting people picked up by local police on any kind of minor or fabricated charge—can only be initiated and regulated by the *federal* government.

But the difference between Judge Pfaelzer and lawyers who represented the State of California goes beyond the question of which level of government has the jurisdiction and authority to coordinate and direct the system's attacks on immigrants. It is connected to the broader argument within the ruling class over how to proceed with the War on Immigrants and other reactionary measures that they are carrying out.

Capitalist Rulers

The anti-immigrant offensive is part of the system's overall *war on the people*. The U.S. capitalists/imperialists are facing intensifying economic competition with their rivals based in Japan and Germany. At the same time the capitalist rulers are faced with an intense financial crisis which has left the U.S. government deep in debt. Their response to this situation has been to launch heartless assaults at every level on the lives of millions of people—from the poorest people in inner cities to immigrants ("illegal" as well as legal) to relatively well-off strata who used to hold privileged jobs in capitalist industry. However, there is also sharp ruling class infighting over how best to carry out these assaults. The gridlock over the federal budget has been one indication of these contradictions within the ruling class.

Similarly, while the capitalist rulers as a whole are determined to press ahead with attacks and cutbacks aimed at immigrants, there is also much debate among them about what actual policies should be adopted by the government. For example, even within the, Republican Party those like Pete Wilson who pushed hard for Prop 187 have been opposed by other forces such as former Reagan cabinet member William Bennett.

There are various issues involved in this debate, including competing interests of different sections of capitalists and disagreements over how to deal with big changes in worldwide capitalist production.

Hardly a Good Policy

Even though Proposition 187 has been blocked in the courts, already, two people afraid to seek [medical] treatment have died. Surely even the most hard-hearted California voters did not anticipate that Proposition 187 would lead to this.

The costs of denying children an education are no less serious. In a state that is already struggling to educate its children properly and fight crime in the streets, it is hardly good policy to throw a couple of hundred thousand children out of school, and to create an atmosphere of suspicion and fear in what are supposed to be places of learning.

Cecilia Munoz, *Christian Science Monitor*, December 27, 1994.

One of the key concerns among the rulers is preventing the kind of widespread protest and opposition that ripped through California and sent tremors around the country in the fall of 1994. Walkouts that began at schools in central Los Angeles spread throughout the entire state. Truck drivers bottled up the famous L.A. freeway system as they caravaned throughout the region. Garment workers staged a walkout and protest march through downtown L.A. shortly before election day. Many teachers, doctors, nurses and administrators pledged their determination to not comply with 187. And on October 16, 1994, about 100,000 people marched through L.A.—the largest protest march ever in southern California.

One of the main elements of Prop 187 was an attempt to turn middle class people into snitches and enforcers for La Migra. But a lot of people in the middle class refused to go along with this reactionary program. Not only was there major social upheaval against 187 among the basic people—especially the youth—but many people in the middle class decided that they would rather break the law and risk jail than go along with the racist, cruel Prop 187.

Powerful forces within the ruling class want to find the ways to carry on the anti-immigrant offensive while cooling out and suppressing the widespread anger and determination that erupted against 187. Judge Pfaelzer's ruling should be seen in this light.

New Federal Attacks on Immigrants

While 187 is being argued over in the system's courtrooms, the War on Immigrants continues to escalate in many different ways. A few weeks after Judge Pfaelzer's ruling, the Clinton administration announced what it considers a big achievement: The U.S. government deported a "record number" of immigrants during 1995. The deportation of 51,600 immigrants during the year amounted to a 15 percent increase over the previous year, and a 75 percent increase over 1990.

The border between the United States and Mexico has been increasingly militarized and turned into a war zone. Children of immigrants are being denied schooling in numerous border towns and in some cities in the U.S. interior. Cities in Illinois and Texas have used "occupancy laws" to conduct campaigns aimed at driving out immigrants. In 1995, the largest series of Migra raids in over a decade resulted in the arrest and deportation of several thousand people from several southern states. A report released by a pro-immigrants rights group in Southern California documented hundreds of cases of discrimination and abuse since 187 was passed. The Los Angeles County Sheriff's Department has begun checking the immigration status of all people taken into custody in the L.A. County Jail, and thousands of people have been deported because of this. According to the INS's own statistics, more than 40 percent of the people deported in August 1995 through this program were guilty of no other "crime" than being in this country without papers.

A basic point in Judge Pfaelzer's ruling is that the primary responsibility for repressing immigrants lies with the federal government. This ruling came *precisely at a time when powerful forces within different branches of the federal government are pressing ahead with deadly new attacks on immigrants.*

Major new anti-immigrant legislation was hammered out early in 1996 in Washington, D.C. President Clinton sent a proposed anti-immigrant law to Congress, and the Republicans countered with proposals of their own. One proposal which has been discussed in a House committee would prevent children who are born on U.S. territory and who have immigrant parents from receiving automatic citizenship. . . .

The essential elements of what is being argued out are clear. A columnist for the *San Diego Union-Tribune* wrote, "Anti-immigrant legislation that in some respects goes further than Proposition 187 has already sailed through committees and is ready for action on the House floor."

The proposals call for building more border fortifications at key locations, bringing the strength of the Border Patrol up to about 10,000 within the next few years, creating "computerized verification program for employment" in the five states with the highest immigrant populations, and cutting the amount of legal immigration drastically. They also call for cutting off federal benefits for legal immigrants and many new citizens, and making it much more difficult for people to sponsor family members for immigration. These measures against legal immigrants will have an immediate, and dramatic, impact: it is estimated that 2.4 million people who have been approved for immigration to the United States but don't yet have visas very likely won't be allowed to enter the country. In California alone, as many as 120,000 legal immigrants could lose up to $196 million in federal education aid, making further education impossible for many. And the *Houston Chronicle* estimated that as much as one-third of the federal cutbacks in Medicare and Medicaid could come from eliminating legal immigrants from many programs. Immigrants without papers are already excluded.

Divide and Conquer

The forces behind Prop 187 claimed that their initiative was only aimed at "illegal" immigrants, not those who have papers. This was nothing but a cynical tactic to create divisions between different sections of the people and to sell the illusion that gaining legal documents or citizenship was the answer—a tactic aimed at weakening resistance to the system's attacks. The steps now being seriously discussed against legal immigrants show how dangerous it is to be sucked into the system's divide-and-conquer schemes.

These new anti-immigrant moves from the federal level are one reason why the forces behind the effort to get 187 passed weren't upset at Judge Pfaelzer's ruling. A spokesman for the most prominent anti-immigrant group, FAIR (Federation for American Immigration Reform), said of the proposed new federal law: "This is a heavyweight, no-nonsense immigration bill—the antithesis (opposite) of 187, which was a grassroots drafting job and reflected it." Another figure in the pro-187 effort said, "The main message [of 187] was to get the federal government off their butts to solve the problem of illegal immigration—and it worked."

And Pete Wilson declared after Pfaelzer's ruling: "Congress has heard our outrage, and they are acting. We are very encouraged by federal law changes advancing through the Congress, and hopeful that when they pass, much of Proposition 187 will become law despite the court's ruling."

Even though official enforcement has been delayed, Prop 187

has already had a big impact on the lives of immigrants—driving many immigrants further into the shadows and stirring up more anti-immigrant poison. The Community Health Foundation in East Los Angeles—an area where many immigrants live—said that since 187 was voted on 40 percent fewer women are seeking early prenatal care at their clinics. This will surely lead to more health problems for women and children.

In September 1995 in Pacoima, near L.A., the outside of an apartment where immigrants live was plastered with the words "go back to Mexico." The *San Jose Mercury News* reported that an immigrant rights attorney in L.A. received "hate mail that superimposed her face on a target with 'open fire' scrawled over it. The letter called the woman . . . 'Latina scum.' Across the top of the page it warned that '187 will be enforced.'" Right-wing militia groups have reportedly called for "armed patriots" to go to the U.S.-Mexico border to help La Migra in suppressing immigrants.

The system clearly intends to intensify its attacks on immigrants across the board. And now, the War on Immigrants is being more openly coordinated and directed from the highest ranks of the central government.

Judge Pfaelzer's ruling on 187 shows why the people should throw away illusions about getting any support from federal courts or any other institution of the system. Far from "striking down" the basic contents of 187, this court ruling is part of the system's efforts to *strengthen and centralize* the War on Immigrants.

The power structure is carrying out a brutal and furious war against the poor. Immigrants—especially those without papers—are being targeted with particularly savage, deadly and systematic assaults.

People who have worked long and hard at many of the most difficult and lowest paying jobs capitalism has to offer are being called "freeloaders." They are being told their kids can't go to school, and they can't go to hospitals. Peasants and workers—whose countries have been ransacked by U.S. imperialism and who are forced to travel far away from home in search of jobs to survive on—are being hunted down like animals along the border. . . .

There is a real and urgent need for people opposed to the system's deadly War on Immigrants to rise to the challenge: To go beyond the levels of struggle and organization which were reached in the outpourings against 187, and bring forth still higher, broader, and more determined levels of resistance to all the attacks on immigrants this system is unleashing.

"Even if moral obligations to illegal aliens exist and are compelling, they by no means imply birthright entitlement to American citizenship."

Repealing Birthright Citizenship Would Be Fair

Peter H. Schuck and Rogers M. Smith

The U.S. Supreme Court has interpreted the Citizenship Clause of the Fourteenth Amendment as granting automatic citizenship to any person born in America. In the following viewpoint, Peter H. Schuck and Rogers M. Smith disagree with this interpretation and contend that the Citizenship Clause should not be interpreted as granting automatic citizenship to native-born children of illegal immigrants. The authors maintain that U.S. citizenship should be based on the mutual consent of society and the individual. Schuck is a professor at Yale University Law School in New Haven, Connecticut. Smith is a political science professor at Yale.

As you read, consider the following questions:

1. What does the principle of ascription hold relevant, according to Schuck and Smith?
2. According to the authors, how many births to illegal immigrants occur annually in the United States?
3. What do the authors propose regarding the right of expatriation?

Abridged from "Consensual Citizenship" by Peter H. Schuck and Rogers M. Smith, *Chronicles: A Magazine of American Culture*, July 1992. Reprinted with permission.

The customary division of national laws of citizenship into the "principles" of *jus soli* (place of birth) or *jus sanguinis* (line of descent) denotes the objective criteria most often used to determine one's citizenship. But the conceptions of political membership that have vied for supremacy in Anglo-American law implicate a different, more fundamental dichotomy—one between the rival principles of ascription and consent. . . .

Ascription and Consent

In its purest form, the principle of *ascription* holds that one's political membership is entirely and irrevocably determined by some objective circumstance—in this case, birth within a particular sovereign's allegiance or jurisdiction. According to this conception, human preferences do not affect political membership; only the natural, immutable circumstances of one's birth are considered relevant. The principle of *consent* advances radically different premises. It holds that political membership can result only from free individual choices. In the consensualist view, the circumstances of one's origins may of course influence one's preferences for political affiliation, but they are not determinative. . . .

Both the ascriptive and consent principles are attractive and problematic in their pure forms. It is tempting, then, to think that the best features of each can be integrated into a coherent law of citizenship without sacrificing some values that we cherish. Doubtless, that hope explains why American law has combined the two and has varied the mix of ascriptive and consensual elements—especially of birthright citizenship and the right of expatriation—over time. But American law has never adequately reconciled these elements; no combination of consent or ascription that is either theoretically satisfying or practically efficacious, especially in light of current conditions, has yet been achieved. For example, two recent and somewhat related developments have begun to place far greater strain on the ideological compromises between ascription and consent in America's citizenship law. The massive increase in illegal migration to the United States and the equally dramatic rise of the welfare state have transformed perhaps the greatest advantage of birthright citizenship from a modern liberal viewpoint—its automatic inclusiveness—into something of a disadvantage. By underscoring the growing practical importance of consent as the chief constitutive political principle of a liberal society, these developments invite us to reconsider birthright citizenship on legal and policy as well as philosophical grounds. They lead us to reject the traditional rule and to propose a more consensualist law of citizenship in which ascribed status at birth plays a correspondingly reduced role.

When the framers of the Fourteenth Amendment's Citizenship

Clause adopted (in a significantly compromised form) the common-law rule of birthright citizenship, immigration to the United States was entirely unregulated. In 1980, the number of illegal aliens in the United States was conservatively estimated at between three and a half to six million, with the number increasing by two hundred thousand annually. Approximately two million of these people will eventually receive legal status under the 1986 amnesty law, but many others did not qualify or have arrived in the years since 1982, the amnesty cutoff date.

No Consent

If mutual consent is the irreducible condition of membership in the American polity, questions arise about a practice that extends birthright citizenship to the native-born children of such illegal aliens. The parents of such children are, by definition, individuals whose presence within the jurisdiction of the United States is prohibited by law and to whom the society has explicitly and self-consciously decided to deny membership. And if the society has refused to consent to their membership, it can hardly be said to have consented to that of their children who happen to be born while their parents are here in violation of American law.

No Automatic Right

Peter H. Schuck and Rogers M. Smith argue that the United States is a society of mutual consent. Citizenship, being at the very basic level of our society, is something that [society and the individual citizen] should consent to, at least implicitly. Clearly, the society as a whole has not consented to the presence of illegal aliens or their children. Therefore, the children of illegal aliens should not receive an automatic right of citizenship simply because they are born here.

Sarah A. Adams, *Immigration Review*, Fall 1993.

The present guarantee under American law of automatic birthright citizenship to the children of illegal aliens can operate, at the margin, as one more incentive to illegal migration and violation by nonimmigrant (temporary visitor) aliens already here of their time-limited visa restrictions. When this attraction is combined with the powerful lure of the expanded entitlements conferred upon citizen children and their families by the modern welfare state, the total incentive effect of birthright citizenship may well become significant. In addition to anecdotal evidence that many aliens do cross the border illegally to assure United States citizenship for their soon-to-be-born children, a recent study illuminates two features of this phenomenon. First, the number of births in the United States to illegal alien parents is not trivial; a conservative estimate places the number as in excess of seventy-five thousand each year. Second, these births—and the public costs that they entail—are disproportionately concentrated in a relatively few urban areas.

Congress has the power to respond to this infringement of consensualism if it so desires. Although the Citizenship Clause of the Fourteenth Amendment has been assumed to guarantee birthright citizenship to such children *ex proprio vigore*, the question of the citizenship status of the native-born children of illegal aliens never arose during its adoption for the simple reason that no illegal aliens existed at that time, or indeed for some time thereafter.

No Universal Rule

The debates also establish that the framers of the Citizenship Clause had no intention of establishing a universal rule of birthright citizenship. To be sure, they intended to do more than simply extend citizenship to native-born blacks by overruling the reasoning and result in *Dred Scott* [an 1857 U.S. Supreme Court decision that declared that blacks were not citizens]. But they also intended, through the clause's jurisdiction requirement, to limit the scope of birthright citizenship. The essential limiting principle, discernible from the debates (especially those concerned with the citizenship status of Native Americans) was consensualist in nature. Citizenship, as qualified by this principle, was not satisfied by mere birth on the soil or by naked governmental power or legal jurisdiction over the individual. Citizenship required in addition the existence of conditions indicating mutual consent to political membership.

Our interpretation certainly does not imply that children of illegal aliens are not entitled to any constitutional protection. Indeed, those children (and perhaps their parents as well) may have legitimate moral or humanitarian claims upon American society. We may be said to have incurred moral obligations to illegal aliens by encouraging them to migrate here, by enriching ourselves through their labor, by absorbing them into our communities, by inviting legitimate expectations of humane treatment, and by other behavior. But even if moral obligations to illegal aliens exist and are compelling, they by no means imply birthright entitlement to American citizenship. Again, that does not mean that policy toward illegal aliens is morally unconstrained. For children who have already been born here of illegal alien parents, for example, a retroactive change in the law depriving them of their citizenship status would violate important expectation and reliance interests and create great confusion and uncertainty.

But these concessions to prudence, fairness, and humanitarianism should not be taken to deny to the American community the essence of a consensual political identity—the power and obligation to seek to define its own boundaries and enforce them. If Congress should conclude that the prospective denial of birthright citizenship to the children of illegal aliens would be a valuable adjunct of such national self-definition, the Constitution should not be interpreted in a way that impedes that effort. Citizenship status is not necessary to afford illegal aliens and their children at least minimal legal protection and public benefits. They do and should possess certain rights by reason of their presence within the United States. Protection against any risk of statelessness can be assured by statute. Thus, the Constitution need not and should not be woodenly interpreted either to guarantee their children citizenship or to cast them into outer darkness.

In the end, the question of birthright citizenship for the children of illegal and nonimmigrant aliens should be resolved in the light of broader ideals of constitutional meaning, social morality, and political community. These ideas militate against *constitutionally* ascribed birthright citizenship in these circumstances. Beyond the issue of the Citizenship Clause's intent, it is morally questionable to reward lawbreaking by conferring the valued status of citizenship, and it is even more questionable to plant that guarantee in the Constitution. This is true even though the lawbreakers are often individuals whose ambition, resourcefulness, and family values most Americans would admire. Those characteristics might lead Congress to confer citizenship broadly and easily, but as a matter of informed choice, not constitutional inadvertence.

A New Law of Citizenship

Basic steps are required to achieve a law of citizenship at birth that is theoretically consistent, practical for addressing current policy problems, and consonant with the nation's fundamental claim that its government rests on the consent of the governed. The first step requires a reinterpretation of the Citizenship Clause of the Fourteenth Amendment. Its guarantee of citizenship to those born "subject to the jurisdiction" of the United States should be read to embody the principle of consensual membership, and therefore to refer only to children of those legally admitted to permanent residence in the American community—that is, citizens and legal resident aliens.

On our consensualist reading, those born "subject to the jurisdiction" of the United States would be citizens at birth provisionally, in the sense that they would have the opportunity upon attaining majority to renounce that citizenship if they so desired. At no time, however, would they be vulnerable to any denial of consent to their membership on the part of the state. Native-born children of legal resident aliens would also be provisional citizens at birth and during their minority and would enjoy the same right to expatriation. Citizenship at birth would not be guaranteed to the native-born children of those persons—illegal aliens and "nonimmigrant" aliens—who have never received the nation's consent to their permanent residence. Even the citizenship law of the United Kingdom, for whose antecedents our common-law citizenship was originally derived, and which continues to adhere to the birthright citizenship principle, does not extend it to the native-born children of either illegal aliens or temporary resident aliens. The same is true of other Western European countries. Since the proposed doctrine would require a reinterpretation of the Citizenship Clause, the change should be made prospectively, assuring citizenship to those born in the United States while the current understanding has been in effect.

Congress, which bears the ultimate responsibility for fashioning the structure of our immigration policy, would also decide the role of the birthright citizenship for the children of illegal and nonimmigrant aliens. That decision is obviously only a small piece of immigration policy. Congress must carefully weigh the moral claims of these children to membership relative to the claims of other groups, assessing the likely effects on illegal immigration of eliminating their present guarantee of citizenship, and considering how such a change should relate to the more comprehensive, systematic measures for reducing illegal immigration. We are genuinely uncertain about how such an evaluation would or should come out. It is an issue on which reasonable people can differ.

Expatriation

The second step necessary to realize a consistent, consensual law of citizenship at birth is to render the right of expatriation more meaningful. We propose that a formal procedure be established and publicized under which any citizen, at the age of majority, may expatriate himself (preserving citizens' rights to do so subsequently as well). Despite recurring calls for legislation fully prescribing formal expatriation procedures, there is no legislated procedure for expatriating oneself within the United States under normal circumstances. As a result few know that an expatriation right exists, and it is procedurally difficult to exercise. In that sense, citizenship is more ascribed than consensual.

We would not only permit native-born citizens to seek another nationality, but would also guarantee them permanent residence in the United States if they wished it. Our proposal would thus retain the asymmetry, created by Supreme Court rulings, between affirming the individual's right to self-expatriation, while denying the nation's power to denationalize those who are already members. Although a thoroughgoing commitment to pure consensual membership might seem to imply a national power to denationalize citizens at will, the existence of such a power might threaten the vigorous exercise of basic constitutional freedoms, such as First Amendment political rights, or might create a condition of involuntary statelessness and thus of acute human vulnerability.

Life Prospects

We have considered a number of objections to our proposal to reinterpret the constitutional guarantee of birthright citizenship. The most troubling objective is that our position does little to address the problem of the influx and status of illegal aliens. Indeed, by eliminating constitutionally mandated birthright citizenship for their native-born children, the proposal could (depending upon the magnitude of its countervailing disincentives to illegal migration) actually increase the number of individuals in illegal status. In this view, the current birthright citizenship rule has at least one virtue that our proposal lacks. It recognizes that in fact (due largely to ineffective immigration enforcement) many native-born children of illegal aliens, along with their parents, will manage to remain here indefinitely. Denying birthright citizenship to those children would add one more obstacle and disadvantage, one more source of stigma and discrimination, to those they must endure as they continue living in American society, as many will be able to do. This dilemma is compounded by the fact that these children's life prospects would be clouded by the action of others over whom they have no control—in this case, the illegal entry of their parents. Better (defenders of the current rule might argue) to eliminate their cruel disability at the moment of birth than to maintain it thereafter.

Although appealing, this argument from life prospects is ultimately unpersuasive. Our proposal to make one's national status turn, at least provisionally, on the national status of one's parents seems more morally acceptable and less determinative of one's life prospects than many other contingent factors—such as inherited wealth, upbringing, or genetic endowment—that are far more likely to shape those prospects in fundamental ways. Indeed, our proposal seems less arbitrary in terms of life prospects than the fundamental concept of birthright citizenship itself, which bases national status wholly upon the accident of geographical location at birth. And even if the innocence of the child and allied concern for his life prospects are accepted as morally or legally relevant, it does not follow that *citizenship*, as

49

distinguished from mere nondiscrimination, should be the prize for that innocence. Nondiscrimination does not necessarily imply the same rights and benefits that citizenship or legal residence status confers. These children and their parents, by being denied birthright citizenship, would not be treated as the *Dred Scott* decision treated blacks; they would not be denied the law's protection. They would instead be required to choose among continuing to live in illegal status, with more limited equal protection and due rights; seeking to obtain legal status; or returning to their home countries.

True Citizenship

Our proposed interpretation would, moreover, produce at least one benefit. The government of a more truly consensual polity could more truthfully proclaim to citizens, resident aliens, and illegal aliens alike that American citizenship stands on a firm foundation of freely willed membership. It could more credibly claim the contemporaneous allegiance and, if necessary, the personal sacrifice of its citizens than it was able to do during the Vietnam War and other corrosive national conflicts. It could more persuasively invoke what it now can only baldly assert—a legitimacy grounded in a fresh, vital, and always revocable consent.

VIEWPOINT

"Birthright citizenship is real citizenship. Better birthright citizenship than racial citizenship."

Repealing Birthright Citizenship Would Be Unfair

Frank H. Wu

In the following viewpoint, Frank H. Wu argues that birthright citizenship is a democratic and proper endowment of U.S. citizenship. Wu contends that birthright citizenship, which he says is more equitable than citizenship based on race, constitutionally protects Americans' citizenship rights. Repealing birthright citizenship would confer an inferior, second-class status on children of immigrants, the author maintains. An assistant law professor at Howard University in Washington, D.C., Wu worked as a campaign organizer with Californians United Against Proposition 187. He writes regularly for the New York Times Syndicate and *Asian Week*.

As you read, consider the following questions:

1. In Wu's opinion, on what basis did U.S. Customs Service agents question his citizenship?
2. What are the "two separate stories" of immigration in America, according to Wu?
3. According to the author, why has immigration again become a contentious issue?

I am a native-born citizen of the United States of America. Under current constitutional doctrine, because I was born here I automatically became an American.

Like most Americans, I usually take my status for granted. But like many Americans, I know that occasionally my right to remain in the country of my birth, along with my right to participate meaningfully and equally in its culture and government, depends on my ability to assert that status. I have had my citizenship challenged enough to believe that in a multiracial society, birthright citizenship is vital to ensuring that our nation of immigrants lives up to its ideal that anyone can become an American.

I am a Midwesterner. I was born in Cleveland, Ohio, and grew up in Detroit, Michigan. When I was growing up, I enjoyed visiting Windsor, Ontario, in Canada, for Chinese food. Many Chinese American families, and Detroit residents of various backgrounds, travel across the Ambassador Bridge on weekends for dim sum or bargain shopping.

Whenever I entered the territory of our northern neighbor, Canadian border guards generally asked a few routine questions and sometimes made a friendly comment about the cuisine. Returning to my homeland, however, can lead to a somewhat different encounter.

Stopped at the Border

A few years ago, when I was a law student, I was stopped by the Customs Service. I was in a car with two other Asian Americans. We also were with another friend of mine, who happened to be Caucasian.

After we were told that we would have to answer a few extra questions, we went inside the main office and waited with about ten other people—all but two of whom looked to be non-Hispanic whites. The officers asked each of us where we had been born and what we did for a living.

For some reason, the agents decided to inquire further with me. They wanted to know, for example, how I had met my white friend, how long we had known one another, and what was the nature of our relationship. Apparently they were satisfied by my answers and released us. The entire incident lasted a quarter of an hour; it was not anything terrible. Afterward, though, I wondered who the Customs Service thought we were and what they thought we were doing. So I wrote to them.

A month later, I received a reply from my government. The official response stated, "Contrary to belief, law enforcement officials, including Customs and Immigration inspectors, cannot distinguish between honorable, law-abiding citizens and violators on the basis of their physical appearance alone."

Of course, they are right. Indeed, that is just the point. You cannot tell the difference between people who are law-abiding and people who could potentially be law-breaking by the way they happen to look. That is why you shouldn't guess, especially when you might be focusing on race, either consciously or unconsciously.

A Matter of Race

Other than race, I cannot think of any difference the Customs Service would be able to identify between me and my white friend that would cause suspicion about citizenship. We have similar social, economic and educational backgrounds (we both eventually became law professors). We speak the same language. We even were dressed alike.

The letter continued, "Many attempts at alien smuggling are made by people posing to be friends to a 'non-suspect' traveler. . . . Even though the questions may seem irrelevant or out of place to you, there is a purpose for asking them."

Unfortunately, that reasoning makes sense only if you accept assumptions about individuals based on their race. While the letter refrains from referring to race, there isn't anything else it offers as the basis for distinguishing between the "suspect" friend and the "non-suspect" traveler. The letter makes no effort to explain why I was suspect and my friend was not. Whatever the reason for asking about the "authenticity" of relationships between people of color and whites, the same purpose should exist for asking similar questions of two whites, if anyone should be asked at all.

Based on my own experiences, I believe that I saw only a small part of a much larger problem. The Customs Service approach reveals that problem, which consists of doubting the citizenship of nonwhites and then trying to excuse or justify racial stereotyping as reasonable or necessary. People who assume that their own American identity is assured may be puzzled by the phenomenon, but I know too many other people who share memories of that embarrassing episode of being asked, "Where are you from?" only to answer, and be asked again, "No, where are you really from?"

With the rise in anti-immigrant sentiment dividing our society further into "us" and "them," more and more Americans can be expected to be interrogated about their identity in this manner. Birthright citizenship provides an essential response. Birthright citizenship is an important means of protecting these citizens as well as keeping the promise of equal opportunity for immigrants.

In this viewpoint, I argue that birthright citizenship must be maintained for three independent reasons. First, as an historical matter birthright citizenship has evolved as the law of the land in the course of repudiating what can be characterized fairly as racial citizenship. Second, as an institution birthright citizenship defines what it means to be an American in the most optimistic and inclusive sense. Third, by a pragmatic analysis birthright citizenship is facing an attack in an overreaction to so-called illegal immigration.

Birth Rights Instead of Racial Rights

The United States of America is unique. We have stated and debated that defining proposition since the founding of the nation. It is as rooted in our shared mythology as the Constitution from which it is derived.

We have attempted to establish our exceptionalism through our immigration policy. Unlike the Old World, a concept encompassing the geographical location as well as the political philosophy from whence our ancestors came, we profess to welcome immigrants of all races. Citizenship in the past and everywhere else still rests on either blood or soil. People are considered citizens because of their race or their birthplace. But it is race that predominates.

In contrast, citizenship here has become idealized. People become citizens because they wish to participate in a great experiment of democracy. Our common ground has shifted from a racial right to be an American toward a birthright to be enjoyed by diverse peoples.

The shift has been incomplete. Like our uniqueness and exceptionalism, our immigration policy is contradicted by our past. Our immigration epic has always consisted of two separate stories. The positive plotline is our tradition of celebrating the arrival and the contributions of innumerable racial and ethnic groups and individuals. Its metaphors are the melting pot, salad bowl, and mosaic. The negative counterpart is our habit of fearing immigrants, warning of their customs, and blaming them for economic difficulties. Its metaphors are a floodtide, an invasion, the Tower of Babel.

Our immigration laws represent our struggle to reconcile these conflicting narratives. But immigration laws are bound up together with other laws. The rules of citizenship have been shaped by the struggle for black civil rights.

The *Dred Scott* Decision

In 1857, the United States Supreme Court decided the notorious case of *Dred Scott v. Sandford*. There, the Court invalidated the Missouri Compromise, which excluded slavery from some territories. As importantly, the Court ruled that individuals of African descent, whose forced emigration is an overlooked chapter of immigration history, were excluded from citizenship.

Few who object to birthright citizenship would concur with the tortuous reasoning of the *Dred Scott* decision or affirm its racist result of denying citizenship to blacks.

After the Civil War, Congress and the States adopted the Fourteenth Amendment, the source of our guarantee of "equal protection" under the law. The Fourteenth Amendment opens with the statement that "all persons born or naturalized in the United States and subject to the jurisdiction thereof, are citizens of the United States and of the State wherein they reside." There was no doubt at the time that the clause overturned the *Dred Scott* decision by both its literal language and legislative intent.

No Solution

The German policy of denying German-born babies their citizenship has not stemmed the flow of immigrants. Indeed, that country has been attracting more immigrants than ever in recent years.

So now, in addition to coping with the problems of mass immigration, the German government also must face a potentially explosive situation: Hundreds of thousands of people born in Germany two or three decades ago still can't vote. They are seething with anger at being excluded politically from the only country they've ever known.

Creating a large class of people with no citizenship will solve no problems in this country either. It will only produce an angry, disenfranchised group of people who live here but lack patriotic feelings.

We need to do something about the growing problem of illegal immigrants, but turning American-born babies into a stateless class is not the way to go.

Marilyn Geewax, *San Diego Union-Tribune*, August 22, 1993.

At the turn of the twentieth century, the Supreme Court confirmed that birthright trumped race. The Court considered the less well-known case of *Wong Kim Ark v. United States*. That case concerned an American-born child of Chinese parents. Although the elders were residents of this country, they were prohibited from ever attaining citizenship by virtue of the Chinese Exclusion Act—legislation which had ended an era of "open borders" at the federal level and begun a series of race-based restrictions on immigration. Their child, however, had been born within the country and had a stronger claim to citizenship. Answering the question of the child's citizenship, a majority of the Supreme Court wrote that the reach of the Fourteenth Amendment was "general, not to say universal, restricted only by place and jurisdiction, and not by color or race."

Taken together, *Dred Scott* and *Wong Kim Ark* render birthright citizenship integral to the development of antidiscrimination principles for all peoples. While overturning the latter case would not necessarily reinstate the former, the implications of eliminating birthright citizenship extend beyond immigration itself to civil rights broadly conceived. Citizens whose status is vulnerable, not least because they are confused with foreigners, are protected by birthright citizenship.

Many Prejudices

Despite the formalism of the law, early twentieth-century popular culture continued to view American as a racial category. As immigration trends shifted toward Southern and Eastern Europe, xenophobes demonstrated a multitude of prejudices. Their attitudes were racial as well as religious, directed at not only Asians and Latinos but also white ethnic groups. Anti-Catholic sentiments and anti-Semitism were voiced loudly in the call to close the borders. The original "America First" crowd felt threatened by every aspect of ethnic behavior. Later arrivals were seen as illiterate and uncultured, criminal and diseased, lazy and stupid, anarchist and communist, but above all, forever unassimilable and therefore un-American. Over time, being "Born in the U.S.A." changed their children, even as their children changed the country.

What It Means to Be an American Today

Birthright citizenship is powerful. Immigrants and citizens are connected through naturalization and the native-born child. Where naturalization is impossible because of racial restrictions, the native-born child alone stands as the legal link between the outsider and the community. It is by birthright citizenship that first-generation Americans are equals, neither foreigners nor guests notwithstanding perceptions.

Perhaps because of its value to successive generations of newcomers, and since it was enshrined in the Constitution, birthright citizenship was accepted for a century. Only in 1986 was it challenged, when professors Peter Schuck and Rogers Smith introduced their academic argument for interpreting the Fourteenth Amendment to mean its contrary. They suggested, following a scholarly review of the historical antecedents for birthright citizenship, that it be abandoned in favor of an abstract notion they called "citizenship by consent."

In *Citizenship Without Consent: Illegal Aliens in the American Polity*, Schuck and Smith argue that birthright citizenship is archaic. It reflects a tendency to stereotype people by ascribing traits to them based on irrelevant characteristics, in this case, the physical location where they were born. Throughout their book, significantly, Schuck and Smith state that they abhor decisions about who can and who cannot become a citizen based on race or ethnicity. They further note that principles protecting racial minorities are an important corollary of their proposal.

Since Schuck and Smith published their idea, though, it has been appropriated by individuals and organizations who seem to share neither their concern about prejudice nor their emphasis on consent. Leading the charge to defend the borders as a point of racial pride is author Peter Brimelow.

Peter Brimelow and Nationalism

Himself proudly an immigrant from England, Brimelow argues in his best-selling polemical tract, *Alien Nation: Common Sense About America's Immigration Disaster*, that birthright citizenship should be gotten rid of, along with almost all immigrants, too. For Brimelow, immigration is more or less the same: illegal or otherwise, it is racially anathema, and almost as an aside, presumed to be economically disadvantageous.

Unlike Schuck and Smith, Brimelow—who peremptorily disclaims that he is not a racist—writes forthrightly about his color-conscious vision of what it means to be an American: "The American nation has always had a specific ethnic core. And that core has been white." To be precise, "the American stew of 1790 . . . for better or worse . . . tasted distinctly British." Accordingly, any immigration that is not racially Caucasian and preferably British, threatens to "break down white America's sense of identity." A fellow proponent of lowering levels of immigration, writer Michael Lind, observed that Brimelow argues for "what looks very much like a defense of old-fashioned white racial nationalism."

Showing the difference between theory and practice, Schuck and Smith invoke consent as the basis for citizenship, but Brimelow evokes racial nationalism. By Brimelow's conception of citizenship, to be an American is to be white. In the political sphere, Schuck and Smith are as obscure as Brimelow is infamous. Consequently, if birthright citizenship gave way to a different understanding, it is likely to lead to a revival of racial citizenship rather than an initiation of consent citizenship. In a postmodern mass culture, citizenship by consent lacks meaning, but divides the country into those who can give consent and those who must seek it.

Equal Citizenship

Simply because some will admit their yearning for a white America, still it would be unwise to defend birthright citizenship by impugning the motives of those who would attack it or by assigning guilt by association. There are robust arguments in favor of birthright citizenship from logic and law.

Our constitutional structure requires birthright citizenship to make citizenship equal for everyone. Immigrants who naturalize, however much we may pretend to grant them full status as citizens, always are regarded as belonging to a different "homeland" and having adopted America. Hence the efforts to strip naturalized citizens of any government entitlements. Anything aside from birthright citizenship risks becoming a second-class status.

Ultimately, immigrants who naturalize gain acceptance by their children, native-born citizens. Even if first-generation Americans born of legal immigrants were deemed citizens by statutory law, they remain thus dependent on legislative grace, which turns on political pressures. If first-generation Americans have citizenship given to them, they will be expected to be grateful. Their citizenship will remain an inferior form. Birthright citizenship is real citizenship. Better birthright citizenship than racial citizenship.

Illegal Immigration Issues

The birthright citizenship controversy should be placed into context. Birthright citizenship has come under fire because of illegal immigration. As the immigration debate has turned into the illegal immigration debate, eliminating birthright citizenship has emerged as an option. Its proponents offer a single rationale for their scheme: they insist that there are hordes of pregnant women from Mexico, who wait until they are ready to give birth to enter this country to bear citizen children. This claim would be laughable if it were not taken seriously.

The illegal immigration problem is perception, not reality. The Immigration and Naturalization Service, no friend of illegal immigrants, estimates that a few million individuals are in the country without documentation, making up about one percent of the total population. Even legal immigrants comprise a lower proportion of the population than they did during the entire period between the Civil War and the Depression.

In fact, the majority of people who are in violation of immigration statutes entered the country legally. They include visiting tourists and foreign students who have overstayed their visas; many are Canadian and Irish. Only a minority cross over the southern border and only a minority are Mexican.

Yet in myth, the illegal immigrant is depicted most often as the migrant worker from Mexico who treks back and forth regularly between his family and his job, sometimes as hundreds of Chinese laborers smuggled professionally in the cargo hold of a ship that has run aground, an entire fleet of Haitian boat people fleeing a repressive regime only to be met by U.S. gunboats on the high seas, or the Arab terrorist who masterminded the bombing of the World Trade Center.

The portrayal of all illegal immigrants as Latinos and other people of color has created the image that all Latinos and racial minorities are illegal immigrants. When people say that they see foreigners all around them, they may well be looking at Latinos and Asians who are fifth-generation Texans or Californians. They know no better than the Customs Service agents who is a citizen and who is the illegal immigrant.

Nonetheless, the illegal immigrant has become the welfare queen of the 1990s. The expecting Mexican mother who sneaks into the country to give birth to a citizen child is a symbolic sister to the unwed African American woman who becomes pregnant to increase her welfare benefits. She is a fictional figure. The single spectacular case, if it even exists, engenders a stereotype. Stereotypes ought not shape public policy.

Whatever their legality, immigrants come to the country because they have connections to it, through friends, family, or employment opportunities. No student of the subject has ever concluded that illegal immigrants enter the country for government entitlements, much less the speculative possibility that their children will obtain welfare benefits. Moreover, citizen children eventually contribute to our economy.

We must consider whether we are prepared to accept the consequences of ending birthright citizenship. Innocent children would be left in limbo if they could not demonstrate the legal status of their parents. The few children who are born in this country of undocumented parents would be forcibly removed with their parents. If we can countenance such treatment of newborn infants in the name of controlling our borders, we will have adopted a siege mentality. We will have accepted that we must prove our citizenship and acquiesced in challenges to it. Even if we wished to reduce illegal immigration, the campaign to end birthright citizenship is foolish.

Immigration has become contentious again because anxieties about the position of whites in this country have blended with worries about the role of the United States in the world. Due to immigration, demographic changes mean that within the foreseeable future, white Americans will find themselves racial minorities like everyone else. The new nativism recalls old themes, but the current conflict also presents us with an opportunity to reject racism and embrace our future together.

Birthright citizenship brings us together. Far from being based on an "accident of birth," it is based on a worthwhile tradition of welcoming immigrants. The accident would be abolishing it.

Periodical Bibliography

The following articles have been selected to supplement the diverse views presented in this chapter. Addresses are provided for periodicals not indexed in the *Readers' Guide to Periodical Literature*, the *Alternative Press Index*, or the *Social Sciences Index*.

Spencer Abraham and Sam Brownback	"Outline of a National Computer I.D. Crisis," *Washington Times*, October 4, 1995. Available from Reprints, 3600 New York Ave. NE, Washington, DC 20002.
Evelina Alarcon	"Anti-Immigrant Racism and the Fight for Unity," *Political Affairs*, April 1995.
Marilyn Bechtel	"Anti-Immigrant Attacks Rising After 187," *People's Weekly World*, June 17, 1995. Available from Long View Publishing, 235 W. 23rd St., New York, NY 10011.
Gary S. Becker	"Prop 187 Is Fine—Now Rewrite Federal Law, Too," *Business Week*, January 9, 1995.
Alex García-Rivera	"Jesus, Mary, and Joseph Were Illegal Immigrants," *U.S. Catholic*, April 1995.
Jack Kemp and Joseph L. Lieberman	"Real Americans, Register Here," *New York Times*, July 25, 1995.
Los Angeles Times	"Ruling on Prop. 187: Court Did What Had to Be Done," November 22, 1995. Available from Reprints, Times Mirror Square, Los Angeles, CA 90053.
John J. Miller and Stephen Moore	"A National ID System," *Policy Analysis*, September 7, 1995. Available from Cato Institute, 1000 Massachusetts Ave. NW, Washington, DC 20001.
NACLA: Report on the Americas	Special section on California's Proposition 187, November/December 1995.
Racefile	Special section on California's Proposition 187, November/December 1995. Available from Applied Research Center, 25 Embarcadero Cove, Oakland, CA 94606.
Anne R. Roschelle	"The Political Mileage of Racism," *Peace Review*, vol. 7, nos. 3/4, 1995. Available from Carfax Publishing, PO Box 25, Abingdon, Oxfordshire, OX14 3UE, United Kingdom.
Peter H. Schuck	"The Message of 187," *American Prospect*, Spring 1995.
Ron K. Unz	"Sinking Our State," *Reason*, November 1994.
Abel Valenzuela Jr.	"California's Melting Pot Boils Over: The Origins of a Cruel Proposition," *Dollars and Sense*, March/April 1995.

Do Illegal Immigrants Harm America?

Chapter Preface

It is commonly argued that illegal immigrants displace many U.S. workers and strain state budgets by consuming public services. Although the number of illegal immigrants can only be roughly estimated, some economists have tried to determine how the illegal immigrant population affects local economies.

In 1982, Rice University economist Donald L. Huddle studied an Immigration and Naturalization Service operation that removed 5,440 undocumented workers from job sites in nine major cities. According to Huddle, "An average of seven U.S. workers applied for each job vacated by an illegal immigrant and about 80 percent of the job openings were filled—at least for a short time—by citizens or legal-alien workers." Huddle's findings support the contention by opponents of illegal immigration that undocumented workers are taking jobs desired by many Americans.

Immigrants' rights activists and others, however, counter that many undocumented workers toil for long hours, under poor conditions, and for well below the minimum wage. They argue that few Americans are attracted to the menial but necessary work that illegal immigrants accept. Experts also cite studies showing that illegal immigrants benefit local economies by paying far more in payroll, sales, and other taxes than the cost of the public services they utilize. One Los Angeles County study found that illegal immigrants pay four times as much in taxes as they receive in government benefits.

The effects of illegal immigration on local economies and on U.S. workers are among the issues debated in the following chapter.

"Many [illegal immigrants] come for two purposes that are both destructive and expensive: to commit crimes or to receive government benefits."

Illegal Immigrants Are Harming America

Michael Huffington

Michael Huffington, a former member of the U.S. House of Representatives from California, lost a bid for the U.S. Senate in 1994. In the following viewpoint, Huffington argues that illegal immigrants are harming America—specifically California—by receiving government benefits, committing crimes, and taking up school and prison space. Welfare benefits should be denied to illegal immigrants, Huffington contends, and criminal aliens should be deported.

As you read, consider the following questions:

1. What is the annual net cost of illegal immigrants to California taxpayers, according to Huffington?
2. According to Huffington, what percentage of those arrested in Los Angeles in 1987 were illegal immigrants?
3. In the author's opinion, how will the North American Free Trade Agreement affect immigration?

America is a nation of immigrants. For over a century a steady stream of new arrivals seeking liberty poured into our country through Ellis Island, under the raised torch of the Statue of Liberty in New York Harbor. Today the great port of entry for immigrants has moved three thousand miles across the country to Los Angeles, California. Unfortunately our greatest city has also become the greatest receiver of illegal immigrants as well.

Effects on California

Illegal immigrants are streaming into California. Many of them come to work, but many also come for two purposes that are both destructive and expensive: to commit crimes or to receive government benefits. Many of the services they receive are mandated by the federal government, and the state of California has little discretion regarding the level of the benefits or who gets them. But the people of California foot the bill all the same, and Washington turns a deaf ear to appeals for relief.

Illegal immigration is a major cause in the overcrowding of our schools and our prisons. Illegal immigration is a key reason for our egregious state health care bill. Illegal immigration contributes significantly to our state government deficit.

Illegal immigration must be stopped. It can be stopped if simple steps are taken at moderate expense. But first we need some politicians who will demand those steps and call attention to all elected officials who do not cooperate.

We do not know with certainty how many illegals live in California or how many are coming in each year. Border controls are extremely porous, but estimates of how porous range widely.

According to the Center for Immigration Studies, over 2.3 million illegals had settled in California as of 1992. Recently, the U.S. Immigration and Naturalization Service estimated that 52 percent of all illegal immigrants settled in California. We have therefore a vast stream of people entering our country illegally, and the stream ends here, in the vast lake of undocumented residents living in California.

Exacting High Costs

The findings of three independent, comprehensive studies suggest that the total net cost of illegal aliens to California taxpayers is at least $3 billion and as high as $5 billion annually. This has helped bring about chronic budget gaps for California. Beginning in 1991, Californians have experienced the three largest state budget shortfalls in American history. Spending on illegal immigrants is out of control. From 1989 to 1993, welfare spending on citizen children of illegals rose 424 percent—a total of $236 million. The California Department of Finance estimates that the state paid out more than $170 million in AFDC [Aid to Families with Dependent Children] benefits for citizen children of illegal immigrants for 1992–93.

California's chronic budget deficit, which led in 1990 to the largest tax increase in California history, would be greatly reduced if these costs of illegals were removed.

An Invasion Costing Billions

Our federal government, required by the U.S. Constitution to maintain our borders against invasion—even an invasion of immigrants—has failed miserably. There are literally millions of illegals in this nation. That they receive billions of dollars annually in aid of various forms is unconscionable—and amounts to an open invitation for others to come here and receive the same largesse.

In September 1993, Joseph F. Delfico testified before a House Republican Research Committee looking into the problem of illegal immigration. An official of the Human Resources Division of the federal General Accounting Office, Delfico placed the combined federal, state, and local cost to the five states most heavily impacted by illegal immigration (California, Florida, Texas, Illinois, and New York) at $2.9 billion per year. Of that total, the federal government was bearing only 19 percent, and California alone was paying $1.7 billion.

John F. McManus, *New American*, January 23, 1995.

Under current policy, we have no way of controlling these costs. Illegals swamp our schools, and federal courts render us powerless to deny them access. Instead we spend huge extra sums on remedial education in English. Illegals enter our hospitals to receive free medical care and federal law bars us from refusing entry.

Right now, it is extremely difficult for a public assistance worker to contact the INS [Immigration and Naturalization Service] to detect who is legal or illegal. On the other hand, law enforcement officials regularly cooperate with INS to find employers who are hiring illegals. In a perverse twist, we concentrate our only serious efforts on finding illegals who are actually working.

Alien Inmates

We can get a snapshot of illegal immigration and crime from two detailed studies done in the Los Angeles area in recent years. In 1992, 11 percent of the inmates in Los Angeles County jails were illegal aliens. Forty percent of these inmates will be arrested again, if recent experience holds. In 1987, 24 percent of the arrests in the City of Los Angeles were of illegal aliens. And yet few felons are deported. This policy costs California taxpayers nearly $420 million each year to keep illegal immigrant convicts in prison.

The understaffed INS loses track of many illegal convicts in the 4,500 state prisons and local jails because INS uses a name-based rather than fingerprint-based identification system, which breaks down when illegals use aliases. An unfortunate result is that many illegal convicts are paroled before INS even realizes they have been arrested.

From 1988 to 1993, only nine illegal immigrant prisoners have transferred from a California prison to one in their native land. A transfer can take place only if the prisoner requests it, his country agrees to take him, the United States agrees to transfer the convict, and penal institutions of each country concur.

Amend the Constitution

Under the current law, every child of an illegal who is born on American soil becomes an American citizen automatically. The parents, and the families of the parents, soon follow. Quickly all barriers—already inadequate—to welfare are swept away.

I have called for a constitutional amendment to change the Fourteenth Amendment, which defines citizenship: "All persons born or naturalized in the United States, and subject to the jurisdiction thereof, are citizens of the United States and of the State wherein they reside."

There has been very little attention to this important clause of the Constitution. Over time, the view has been accepted that anyone born here, whether by accident or in contravention of the law, is automatically a citizen.

Now, in a groundbreaking essay, Professor Edward Erler of California State University provides powerful evidence that the children of illegals are not meant to become citizens merely because they are born here.

One example shows how the framers of the amendment spoke of the matter. Senator Jacob Howard—who wrote the citizenship clause in the Fourteenth Amendment—said on May 30, 1866:

> Every person born within the limits of the United States, and subject to their jurisdiction, is by virtue of natural law and national law a citizen of the United States. This will not, of course, include persons born in the United States who are foreigners, aliens, who belong to the families of ambassadors or foreign ministers accredited to the Government of the United States, but will include every other class of persons.

This explicit statement fits with our own common sense. No serious person could believe that the framers of the amendment

66

intended for every person born here to enjoy citizenship.

It is time for politicians to understand the real meaning of the Constitution. I will support legislation giving effect to the real meaning of the Constitution. Children of illegals will no longer automatically become citizens of the United States.

Taking Action

President Bill Clinton has turned a deaf ear to California's appeals for help with the cost of illegals.

I will take action: I have given strong support to the North American Free Trade Agreement, which will create jobs in the United States and Mexico. This will make it possible for Mexicans to find jobs in their own country, and the more Mexicans employed in Mexico, the fewer who will come across the border illegally looking for work. In addition, I will work to stem the tide of illegals. Welfare benefits must be denied to illegals. Illegals convicted of crimes must be deported. And illegals born in this country should not be granted automatic citizenship.

"The real point is that there isn't any immigration crisis."

Illegal Immigrants Are Not Harming America

Richard Rayner

In the following viewpoint, Richard Rayner asserts that there is no immigration crisis in America and that illegal immigrants are not overrunning the border. Rayner maintains that illegal immigrants benefit the U.S. economy and perform jobs that U.S. citizens refuse to do. The author contends that most Americans welcome hard-working illegal immigrants who seek to become part of American life and that most Americans reject strict measures against such immigrants and their American-born children. Rayner is a Los Angeles-based writer and author of the novel *The Blue Suit*.

As you read, consider the following questions:

1. What are the only public benefits available to illegal immigrants, according to Rayner?
2. According to Rayner, what issues does immigration impinge on?
3. Why have pro-immigration forces focused on economic issues, in the author's opinion?

Excerpted from Richard Rayner, "What Immigration Crisis?" *New York Times Magazine*, January 7, 1996. Copyright © 1996 by Richard Rayner. Reprinted with the permission of the Wylie Agency, Inc.

Maria T. bites her nails. At 31, with five children, she's one of the 1.7 million immigrants now estimated to be living in California illegally. She speaks almost no English, even though she has been in America for more than eight years. . . .

"At first I had to beg for food. Sometimes I did day work for Latinos, for $10 a day. I'd take off into the city on the bus, not really knowing where I was going, and get off to beg on the streets. I'm ashamed of that."

Slowly, she clawed her way up. It is in so many ways a classic immigrant's tale, although she has been the beneficiary not just of her own drive, but also of something equally important—welfare. She's here illegally, with fake ID, and she doesn't work. She receives $723 in cash and $226 in food stamps, and Section 8 takes care of more than two-thirds of her $1,000 rent (high, because landlords know illegals won't complain).

Benefits and Taxes

It's a myth, however, that anyone can come over the border and start milking the system. Only Medicaid and limited food benefits are available to illegal immigrants, and most don't apply for these because they fear detection by the Immigration and Naturalization Service [I.N.S.]. Maria T. gets what she does because of those of her children who were born here.

Local, state and Federal Governments spend about $11.8 billion a year educating legal and illegal immigrant children, according to the Urban Institute, a nonpartisan research organization, compared with the $227 billion spent to educate all children. Generally, this is more than offset by the taxes that legal and illegal immigrant families pay—$70.3 billion a year, the Urban Institute says—while receiving $42.9 billion in total services. Illegal immigrants pay $7 billion in taxes.

Maria T., however, represents the nightmare scenario—an illegal immigrant who's sucking money from the system and putting nothing back. Even so, it's not clear that she's a villain. She hopes one day to go to work herself. She hopes and believes that her bright children will become outstanding. She believes in America. . . .

Preserving America

Many have drawn a line behind which they stand, *true* Americans, fearful and angry about the erosion of their identity. With unintended irony they talk of themselves as "natives." On immigration, they argue that enough is enough, that the borders must be secured and a drastic cutback enforced. Those who are allowed in, they say, must be professionals or skilled workers because the others—mobs of unskilled, third-world peasants— drain resources and take jobs. They cost billions and dilute the gene pool. They are mutating the face of America.

California itself, for instance, passed an anti-immigrant measure with scary ease. In 1994's state election nearly 60 percent voted for Proposition 187, the so-called Save-Our-State initiative, which sought to deny public education, nonemergency health care and welfare to illegal immigrants. By linking illegal immigration to joblessness and crime, Pete Wilson revived his flagging gubernatorial campaign and was swept back into office, even though, as an exit poll showed, few who voted for 187 actually thought it was going to work. . . .

The anti-immigration forces have done an excellent job of creating an atmosphere of crisis in which the debate has focused on *how* to slow the "flood" of immigration, legal and illegal. But illegal immigration should not be folded over to scapegoat legals as well. The real point is that there isn't any immigration crisis. . . .

Immigration by Numbers

"The perception is that immigration is out of control," says Joel Kotkin, author of *Tribes* and a fellow at the Pepperdine University Institute of Public Policy. "It isn't. If you say to most Americans, 'We have 800,000 legal immigrants a year,' they're going to reply, 'Hey, that's not so bad.' And this is the truth of the situation. But it's somehow been demonized so that people think there are millions coming across the border."

The Border Patrol logged 1,094,718 apprehensions in 1994. On page 26 of his *Alien Nation*, a leading restrictionist, Peter Brimelow, writes that legal immigration is "overwhelmed by an estimated 2 to 3 million illegal entries into the country in every recent year." He goes on to note, correctly, that many of these illegal entrants go back home, and that some trundle to and fro across the border every day. By page 33, however, he's writing "a remarkable 2 to 3 million illegal immigrants may have succeeded in entering the country in 1993."

Within seven pages illegal entrants have mysteriously become illegal immigrants, attached to that hyperbolic two to three million, a figure vigorously disputed by I.N.S., which regards as preposterous the idea that for every border crosser caught another three get away. Indeed, throughout the 1970's there were some eight million border apprehensions and during that time, according to the best estimates of I.N.S., about one million illegals came to reside—eight apprehensions per illegal immigrant.

So how many illegals are coming in and staying each year now? The Urban Institute says 250,000 to 300,000. The Center for Immigration Studies, a conservative research group, says 400,000, while I.N.S. says 300,000. The Census Bureau until recently guessed 200,000 to 400,000; now it agrees with the I.N.S. The 300,000 figure is considered firm because it was based on the years following 1988, when the I.N.S. started to process the genuinely reliable data it amassed following the 1986 amnesty for illegals. Too much of this and the eyes glaze over, but the gist is, the further you get from 1988, the flakier the statistics become. And the argument over the number of illegal immigrants is nothing compared with the furor over how much they cost.

The fact is, no one knows for sure; there is simply no up-to-date research. "The issue has caught political fire," Carnegie Endowment for International Peace immigration expert Demetrios Papademetriou says. "But serious academics haven't got out into the field yet. They're reluctant to play into the hands of the politicians."

National Issues

Immigration is in the spotlight not because of money but because it so impinges on issues like race, the role of government, national identity and change. Name an issue and you can hook it to immigration. One side looks at crime, failing schools and soaring welfare spending and sees too many immigrants. The other sees America, the greatest nation on earth, built on the backs of immigrants and still benefiting enormously from the brains, energy and determination (not to speak of low wages) of the next generation of newcomers. Right now the debate is more emotional than informed. It's all temper tantrums and red-hot sound bites. . . .

America Is Not Being Overrun

According to a 1994 *Utne Reader:* "The rate of immigration relative to the nation's base population is far below historic levels. . . . Moreover the percentage of foreign-born people in the U.S. population has fallen from 8.89 in 1940 to 6.8 today."

America's not being overrun after all.

"It's true that we're changing to a more international place," says [Museum of Photographic Arts director Arthur] Ollman. [Ollman organized the San Diego exhibit "A Nation of Strangers."] "Americans will become more polyglot. The melting-pot metaphor doesn't work anymore. It's a mosaic. But we're not being overrun, and I find it almost offensive this idea that America is no longer strong enough to handle its immigrant influx.". . .

America's Changing Identity

Pro-immigration forces have tended to keep their focus tight on the economic issues because they sense that Americans don't want to be told they're racist. Nobody does. Yet, one of the problems with the immigration issue is that it *does* impinge on the race issue, and thus appeals temptingly and dangerously to the worst side of all of us.

A central argument of Brimelow's *Alien Nation* is that America has always had an essential nature, an ethnic core, and that it's white. He writes that "the first naturalization law, in 1790, stipulated that an applicant must be a 'free white person.' Blacks became full citizens only after the Civil War."

He goes on: "Maybe America should not have been like this. *But it was.*" And now: "Americans are being tricked out of their own identity."

Reading this, I'm overcome with a weird looking-glass giddiness. Someone's trying to change the rules here, to wipe a rag over history. America's identity is precisely that of mutation, its power drawn from an energetic and quite fearless ability to adapt and win. Its national book, after all, is *The Adventures of Huckleberry Finn*, about a beautiful and dangerous river that never stops changing.

© Matt Wuerker. Used with permission.

America is an immigrant nation; indeed, a nation of strangers. I like it that way, though the arguments in favor of the idea are not merely sentimental and historical. Corporate interests value immigration for something that troubles us—keeping wages lower, and these days not just at the level of busboys and dayworkers.

The American economy is in relatively good shape and has pretty much the legal immigration it needs. The system isn't broken, doesn't need fixing—and certainly not in the ways that were being proposed [by immigration reform advocates in 1996]. Illegal immigration is touchier. Listening to academics makes it easy to forget the racially inflamed brush fire that is the debate in California.

Public Sympathy

Polls show a surprising sympathy even for illegal immigrants, provided they otherwise play by the rules: work, get documentation, learn English. Only 20 percent say immigrants take jobs away from citizens, and 69 percent say they do work that citizens don't necessarily want and that needs to be done. Few say that the American-born children of illegals should be deprived of education and welfare, let alone their citizenship. The message here is a sensible one: beef up the Border Patrol; deport criminals; don't break up families; target labor-enforcement at bad-guy sweatshop employers and make an effort to deal with temporary visa overstays, who surprisingly make up as much as 50 percent of all illegals; supply Federal assistance to heavily impacted areas such as Los Angeles, and forget the idea of a national verification system or an identification card.

Ultimately, this is a debate about values, not money. This is about how America feels about itself.

"The net costs of public assistance for illegal immigrants and the U.S. workers they displace will be between $207 and $280 billion . . . for the decade 1995–2004."

Illegal Immigrants Are an Economic Burden

Donald L. Huddle

Many critics argue that illegal immigrants in America take jobs away from U.S. citizens and take advantage of social services. In the following viewpoint, Donald L. Huddle argues that illegal immigrants drain billions of dollars from many sectors of government and the economy. Huddle contends that U.S. policies contribute to this growing crisis. Huddle is a professor emeritus of economics at Rice University in Houston.

As you read, consider the following questions:

1. What percentage of illegal immigrants are low-skilled, according to INS data cited by Huddle?
2. According to Huddle, which states bear the greatest burden from illegal immigrants?
3. How do asylum-seekers become illegal immigrants, according to the author?

Excerpted from Donald L. Huddle, "The Net National Costs of Illegal Immigration into the United States," Current World Leaders *International Issues*, vol. 38, no. 2, April 1995. Reprinted by permission of the publisher, Current World Leaders *International Issues*, International Academy at Santa Barbara, 800 Garden St., Suite D, Santa Barbara, CA 93101-1552; (800) 530-2682; fax: (805) 965-6071; e-mail: iasb@igc.org.

Rising public concern over the fiscal costs of immigration at both national and local levels has intensified a search for political and administrative answers. Major states of immigration settlement—California, Texas, Florida and New York—are pressing Washington in the courts and in Congress for reimbursement of the costs to them of public assistance to rising numbers of illegal immigrants due to federal indifference and inaction. Pressed to find new savings, Congress has tightened eligibility conditions for some immigrant public assistance programs. . . .

The Social Costs of Job Displacement

According to the Council of Economic Advisers in their 1994 report to President Clinton, between 1981 and 1990 about two million full-time workers per year lost their jobs. These workers spent an average of 30 weeks unemployed, and of those who found new employment one-third lost more than 20% of prior earnings. The impact of job loss was much greater, however, for the low-skilled and less educated. The real income of the bottom 60% of American families was more than 20% lower by the early 1990s than 20 years earlier. By 1993 those with less than a high school education had a 12.5% unemployment rate compared with 3.5% for those with a college degree. Those with a high school degree had an unemployment rate of 7.2% compared with about 2% for those with advanced and professional degrees. The 8.7 million unemployed lost $197 billion in wages in 1993 alone, about 7% less than in 1992, a recession year. A major part of the loss was sustained by low-skill labor.

In 1982, federal payments to a displaced worker with dependents averaged around $7,000. By 1993, the annual cost for an unemployed worker who qualified for Medicaid, Aid to Families with Dependent Children (AFDC), food stamps, unemployment compensation, and general assistance had risen to more than $11,000.

The question is: how much unemployment was caused by displacement and what was the cost? We begin by asking how many illegal aliens were residing in the United States by 1994? The exact number is unknown, but estimates by the INS [Immigration and Naturalization Service], the Census Bureau, and the Center for Immigration Studies (CIS) place the number at between 4 and 5.4 million. INS data indicate that approximately 86% of the undocumented are low-skilled and that 77% are working. Thus, 2.65 to 3.58 million illegals by these estimates are working in low-skill jobs in the U.S. as of 1994. Given that the overall U.S. unemployment rate was lower than the norm during the 1994 economic recovery, we further conservatively estimate at the current time a displacement rate of 25%, i.e., each 100 working low-skill illegals displace 25 U.S. low-skill workers. Then between 663,000 and 894,000 U.S. workers were displaced during 1994. The final adjustment accounts for the fact that not all displaced workers actually qualify for Medicaid and other social programs. Thus, we lower per capita program costs by using only the average utilization rate for each program by the unemployed and arrive at an adjusted total cost of $3.6 to $4.6 billion in 1994 due to displacement.

While $3.6 to $4.6 billion is not a huge number compared with the total losses of the 8.7 million unemployed, we must remember that it represents only the public service costs of displacement, i.e., what it costs the U.S. taxpayer. The displaced worker himself loses many times this amount in wages and benefits. Nor is this the end of the story, for the undocumented also consume public resources that must now be accounted for.

The Costs of Public Assistance

It is true that some federal and state programs are off limits to the undocumented. But others are not. For example, in the Texas School Case *Plyler v. Doe, Guardian, et al.*, five of nine justices of the U.S. Supreme Court ruled that children of illegal aliens had a constitutional right to a free public education. Free public education includes not only primary–secondary education for the undocumented, but also for the "citizen children" of illegal immigrants, i.e., children born to illegal aliens residing in the United States who become citizens by right of birth here. Illegal aliens and their children are also eligible for other education-related programs including student aid, public higher education, school lunch, AFDC, compensatory education, Head Start, adult education, and bilingual education.

Illegal aliens with citizen children also qualify for food stamps; housing assistance; women, infants, and children (WIC); unemployment compensation; job training; Medicaid; the earned income tax credit; and general assistance. Illegal aliens also cause other costs such as criminal justice and corrections, the costs of federal and state highway maintenance, social security for the injured and disabled (SSI); and costs of county and city services—health, police, fire, libraries, parks and recreation, judicial, legal, highways, sewage, welfare, and administration.

As part of a broader study for Carrying Capacity Network, a nonprofit, nonpartisan organization devoted to the study of environmental and population issues, the education, social cost, and incarceration costs of illegal aliens and their citizen children was estimated for the year 1993. The study used a wide variety of federal and state government documents, such as the 1990 Census, the Statistical Abstract of the U.S., the Economic Report to the President, the Digest of Education Statistics, and U.S. Department of Commerce data among many others, to determine the cost of illegal immigration by each cost category. For example, the cost of primary–secondary education was found to be $4.4 billion in 1993. This was determined by using the national per capita cost of K–12 education of $6,336 for a school-age population of illegals of 689,520 (80% of school-age illegals). Using census data once again, we determined that there were 557,940 school-age citizen children, of whom 446,352 were actually in school according to the 1990 Census, costing a total of $2.8 billion. This same procedure was followed for some 25 cost categories with appropriate modifications of data for each public service.

More Reliance on Public Assistance

Where more direct data were not available, the actual recipiency rate of immigrants—for example the 1990 Census showed that 86% of noncitizen immigrant children attended school K–12—was adjusted by the actual immigrant public assistance recipient rate of 44.2% from the 1990 Census. This means that immigrants, on average, receive 44.2% more public assistance weighted by the frequency of receipt and the amount of assistance received than does the remainder of the U.S. population. For example, the 52.5% of school-age population getting free school lunch was increased to 75.7% of school-attending illegals due to their greater poverty and public service recipiency rates.

Using a similar methodology, the total of all public service costs for illegal aliens and their citizen children was calculated to be between $19.6 and $26.5 billion depending upon whether we apply the INS estimate of 4 million illegals or the CIS estimate of 5.4 million illegals, the latter including 550,000 citizen children. The most costly individual programs were public education, $5.6 to $7.6 billion; county and city services, $5.8 to $7.8 billion; social security, $2.6 to $3.5 billion; and bilingual education, $1.3 to $1.7 billion. From the $19.6 to $26.5 billion total must be subtracted all city, county, state, and federal taxes paid by the undocumented totaling $7.6 to $10.3 billion. Total costs minus the total taxes paid in results in total net costs of between $12 to $16.2 billion. When public service costs are added to the average $4.1 billion displacement costs for U.S. workers the overall total cost range is then between $15.6 and $20.8 billion in 1994.

Projecting Future Costs

The Carrying Capacity Network study also projected the future costs of illegal immigration to the United States. By assuming no changes in policy or enforcement, the nation's illegal immigrant population was projected to rise from 5.1 million to 8.1 million by the year 2003.

The Carrying Capacity Network study conservatively projects

that the stock of illegal settlers will grow by an average of 300,000 per year based on current estimates of the Immigration and Naturalization Service. These figures represent the net growth of the stocks of illegal immigrants after taking into account projected emigration and death rates of 1.5% and .5%, respectively. It is also assumed that tax collections will grow by 4.87% annually and that the skill profile of illegal immigrants entering after 1993 and the displacement factor of 25% will both continue.

There is considerable evidence, however, that would support even higher projections of illegal immigration than these if current policies are continued. For example, the Center for Immigration Studies finds that there were 1.21 million immigrants nationally in 1992, if asylum entrants are included (given that about two-thirds of asylees become, de facto, illegal immigrants by not appearing for their hearings). The Center expects this number to continue rising along with total immigration. The Census Bureau's 1992 high projection of all immigration is 1.37 million annually by 2080. Demographers Dennis Ahlburg and James Vaupel find total immigration rising to 2 million by 2080. The INS itself raised its own estimate of illegal immigration from 200,000 yearly to 300,000 yearly. Further increases may well be in store for the U.S. given deteriorating economic and political conditions in Mexico and the Third World.

Using our previous estimates of illegal alien stocks of 4 to 5.4 million and growth by 300,000 yearly, we find that the net costs of public assistance for illegal immigrants and the U.S. workers they displace will be between $207 and $280 billion in present value 1994 dollars for the decade 1995–2004. . . .

Clearly, the current and prospective costs of education and public assistance for illegal immigrants, their citizen children, and those they displace is a massive diversion of federal and state resources from alternative investments with greater potential return. Hardest hit by the state and local shares of these costs are California, New York, Texas, Florida, New Jersey, and Illinois, where nearly 80% of illegal immigrants settle. Since the late 1980s the federal government has actually cut back its contribution to state-run assistance programs to refugee and other humanitarian entrants, while increasing the numbers admitted.

Other Costs and Benefits

Obviously the major driving force behind illegal immigration is jobs for the illegal him or herself and a hard working, compliant, nonunion labor force for the employer—a labor force that insures lower costs and higher profits for employers. Survey data indicate that illegal immigrants also come for a better life for both themselves and their children, including a better education. Many illegals who originally came just to earn money change their objectives as they are in the U.S. longer and assimilate to the blue-jean and fast food culture and the possibility of upward mobility.

Pro-immigration advocates have often pointed out that by benefiting the employer's bottom line, and by spending their earnings in the U.S., illegals also help to create jobs. George Borjas, an immigration researcher and professor of economics at the University of California at San Diego, finds that immigrants, legal and illegal, probably contribute about $6 billion net income yearly to the U.S. economy. This is less than one-tenth of 1% of our $6 trillion gross national product (GNP).

Borjas finds two offsetting effects. First, he estimates that native-born workers lose $114 billion a year from immigrant competition for jobs in the way of wage depression. On the other hand, employers and owners of capital gain about $120 billion per year from the same wage effect. This class of winners includes the more affluent middle class who hire immigrants for nannies, gardeners, and home remodeling jobs.

The above income effects are for all immigration, legal and illegal. Illegal immigrants constitute almost 25% of all immigrants arriving since the year 1969. Thus, the gross wage loss imposed by them on the native-born would be about $28.5 billion and the gain they yield to their employers and the affluent would be about $30 billion. The overall net gain to employers in the private sector minus the losses of native-born employees due to illegal immigration is the difference of $1.5 billion.

However, this overall net gain to the economy of $1.5 billion is more than offset by the public service, education, and incarceration costs of illegal immigrants of between $15.6 and $20.8 billion yearly, resulting in an overall loss for both public and private of between $14.1 and $19.3 billion as of 1994.

Environmental Costs

Among other costs not included up to this point are costs related to the environment, which accompany population growth. These include costs of compliance with clean air and clean water acts, preservation of wetlands, and toxic waste disposal. One example of such costs that the Carrying Capacity Network study was able to determine was the uncompensated environmental and resource costs of operating motor vehicles. These costs, estimated at $.30 per mile by the Todd Littman study in 1993, are projected to total $2.8 to $3.8 billion in 1994 dollars, depending upon whether the resident population of illegals is 4 million or 5.4 million, and are projected to total between $31.2 and $42.2 billion over the 1994 to 2004 decade.

Adding the environmental costs of driving to the prior national deficit results in an overall private, public, and environmental cost of between $16.9 and $23.1 billion in 1994 and approximately $175 billion to $240 billion over the 1994 to 2004 decade.

Other costs not addressed in the current study would add billions more to the above totals. The major costs not quantifiable at the current time are: the costs of public assistance obtained by ineligible immigrants through fraud; the costs of screening, admitting, and administering illegals in federal Departments of Justice, Health and Human Services, Labor, and State; costs in border communities and states of subsidized education for foreign commuter students illegally receiving residential tuition rates in public school and colleges; the value of income taxes and other non-FICA [Social Security] taxes foregone because of the unemployment of displaced U.S. workers and due to depressed wages, or the costs of retraining and relocation aid to them; other environmental costs including the compliance costs of the clean air and water acts, preservation of wetlands, and disposal of toxic waste; finally we have not added the costs to which all legal residents contribute: national defense, national parks, interest on the national debt, and subsidies to government enterprises.

Avoiding Future Costs

It is by now obvious that the current high levels of illegal immigration are costly to the taxpayer. In the private sector, there is a trade-off. The affluent middle class and owners of capital gain substantially from the cheap labor of illegal aliens. Competing laborers, particularly the low-skill, non-college workers, lose out from displacement and wage depression, more than offsetting the private sector's gains. The public sector losses are very large while the private sector gains and losses are more or less offsetting. But, while largely offsetting, the private sector changes greatly worsen the income distribution between the "haves" and the "have nots." This increasing gap exacerbates an already bad situation arising from the continuing internationalization of the economy and rapid technological change, both influences that have caused the loss of millions of high-wage factory and industrial jobs in the U.S. Reflecting these changes, U.S. income distribution is at its most unequal level since such statistics have been kept. The lowest one-fifth of the population now receives only 4.4% of aggregate income while the top one-fifth receives 44.6%.

In poll after poll large majorities of Americans, including native-born and Hispanic immigrants, want to curtail illegal immigration. This has not happened. The major governmental attempt to control and reduce illegal immigration was the Immigration Reform and Control Act (IRCA) in 1986. IRCA was a compromise: more than three million former illegal aliens who had been residents in the U.S. since before 1982 were given amnesty. This included almost a million special agricultural workers (SAWs) who received special dispensation for having worked in United States seasonal agriculture for at least six months. The latter were needed, it was argued by powerful agricultural interests, to insure that the crops didn't spoil in the fields. The trade-off was that business interests allowed an employer-sanctions bill to pass. This required employers to request identification from all new workers hired to insure their legality, or else face stiff fines. To make the system workable, the border patrol and INS were to receive adequate resources to keep our borders secure and to check the documentation of new business hires.

Major Federal and State Benefit Programs Used by Immigrants

Aid to Families with Dependent Children (AFDC)
Supplemental Security Income (SSI)
General Assistance
Housing and Urban Development (HUD)
Community Development Grants
Foster care, adoption assistance, and child welfare
Medicaid, emergency services and services for pregnant women
State and local medical care
School lunch and breakfast programs
Headstart
Job Training Partnership Act
Title IV for Higher Education
Block grants for social services
Adult Education Grants
Women, Infants and Children (WIC) and other child nutrition
Home Energy Assistance

Source: Congressional Research Service of the Library of Congress

Immediately after IRCA passed, the numbers of illegal aliens apprehended at the border dropped precipitously—from almost 1.8 million in 1986 to 1.2 million in 1987 and 950,000 by 1989—as potential illegal entrants waited to see if the new system would work effectively. However, by 1990 border apprehensions were once again on the rise, reaching 1.3 million in 1993, 95% of whom were of Mexican origin, as the government failed to provide sufficient resources to the INS and border patrol. Both continued to be underfunded while factories churned out millions of fraudulent identification documents. Although most employers dutifully kept new employee records as required by IRCA, INS had few investigation teams to check documents for authenticity. Subsequent research showed that massive fraud had occurred in the SAW program as illegal aliens in great numbers crossed the border to claim special agricultural employment status *after* IRCA had passed. According to subsequent INS investigators, perhaps two-thirds of the SAW applicants were fraudulent. In the meantime, the government has yet to develop or test a fraud-proof identification system even though this was required under IRCA itself.

Out of Control

Thus, years after IRCA, the system is moving further out of control with illegal immigration climbing dramatically by 50% to more than 1.3 million in just four years, forcing even the conservative Census Bureau to raise its estimate of permanent resident illegal aliens inflow by 50% from 200,000 to 300,000 yearly.

Border apprehensions are only one part of the problem. Up to 50% of illegal immigration occurs not at the border, but by legal entry and then by visa overstays. In the meantime, another leak has occurred in the system: asylees, a small problem as recently as 1987 when only 25,000 of them arrived, are arriving in ever-increasing numbers—144,000 in fiscal 1993 alone. The problem is that asylees cannot be held until their formal hearings due to a budget shortfall and subsequent lack of INS facilities. Typically asylees are released with a work permit and given a hearing date often well into the future. There is currently a huge and growing backlog. Only 34,000 claims were adjudicated in 1993, with 244,000 or more waiting for hearings. Even then about two-thirds of asylees do not appear at their hearings. Thus, they become de facto illegal immigrants secure in the knowledge that under current immigration policy it is highly improbable that they will be apprehended and deported. Only 36,686 illegal aliens were actually deported in 1993, less than 1% of those residing here even by the conservative Census Bureau estimates.

An Increasing Flow

And matters are likely to become worse. Instead of the improvement in jobs and incomes in Mexico and reduced illegal immigration that supporters of the North American Free Trade Agreement (NAFTA) promised, the agreement instead opened the wallets of banks and investors in the United States and Europe while stripping away the import protection used by Mexico to keep a stable peso. Internal strife in [the state of] Chiapas and the assassination of Institutional Revolutionary Party (PRI) presidential candidate Luis Colosio there were factors that exposed an overvalued peso and, in just a few weeks, a financial crisis developed with peso devaluations greater than 40%. The U.S. has responded with credits in the billions and a promise by the Clinton administration of a credit bailout amounting to over $40 billion. [In 1995, the United States agreed to provide up to $20 billion as part of a $50 billion international bailout.] But many members in Congress express doubts that the bailout is appropriate unless Mexico brings its own monetary excesses to a halt and institutes permanent monetary and democratic reforms.

Whether the U.S. did or did not cosign and arrange $40 billion of Mexican government credits did not signify, as the Clinton administration has claimed, a world-shaking economic conflagration event. What it does mean is an increasing flow of illegal entrants, a flow already in the hundreds of thousands annually due to a toothless U.S. border policy and the Mexican government's yanking away from small farmers millions in credits and price supports even as cheap U.S. farm products swamp Mexico under NAFTA's low tariffs. The net result: millions of Mexican small farmers and their families will immigrate to Mexican cities and the U.S. Only now, these immigrants will be joining hundreds of thousands of other Mexican laborers, tradesmen, and small businessmen unable to make a living wage.

"It is estimated that [illegal immigrants] pay more money in taxes than they receive in social services."

Illegal Immigrants Are Not an Economic Burden

Frank Sharry

In the following viewpoint, Frank Sharry maintains that illegal immigrants are hard workers who use few government services. Sharry contends that illegal immigrants are unjustly blamed for America's economic problems. He insists that the number of illegal immigrants entering the United States and the extent of their dependence on social services are greatly exaggerated. Sharry is the executive director of the National Immigration Forum, an advocacy organization in Washington, D.C.

As you read, consider the following questions:

1. According to Sharry, what percentage of illegal immigrants come from Mexico?
2. In the author's opinion, what is the effect of policies targeting illegal immigrants already in the United States?
3. Where does the majority of illegal immigrants' taxes go, according to Sharry?

The debate over immigration into the United States has heated up considerably. The covers of national magazines showcase the growing backlash against immigrants and the growing diversity of our population. Television and news accounts trumpet dramatic events, new policy proposals and the latest opinion poll. In fact, polls suggest the majority of Americans favor reducing the number of immigrants and refugees admitted to the country. They also make clear that Americans are confused about basic facts and actual effect of newcomers on society.

As the debate intensifies, the issue of illegal immigration is emerging as a primary focus of national concern and policy debate. Some argue our borders are out of control, that too many people are entering the United States illegally and that they are costing Americans jobs and taxes. They argue we should "cut off the magnet" of services, even if it means denying emergency medical assistance to undocumented immigrants and denying K–12 public school admission to undocumented children. Some promote the idea of a national identification scheme in which those who reside in the United States illegally are denied employment and services.

Others argue the problem of illegal immigration is wildly exaggerated, and that some politicians and interest groups are using fear tactics to win votes and raise money. They say undocumented immigrants are freedom-seeking risk-takers who take jobs American workers refuse and avoid using government services for fear of being detected and deported. They view efforts to drive undocumented immigrants out of the country as an ugly outgrowth of anti-immigrant sentiment, which is based less on a careful analysis of real problems, and more on economic uncertainty, racial fears and mean-spirited scapegoating.

How can the uninitiated make sense out of this controversial and emotional debate?

What the Facts Are

First, let's start by asking the right questions: What are the facts about numbers, composition and impacts of immigrants, and in particular, those who enter illegally? Do they take jobs, reduce wages and drain budgets as some claim? Or do they stimulate economic growth by working hard, keeping certain industries competitive and avoiding government services? What is the impact of immigrants, especially those who are here illegally, on state governments? Finally, what can be done to address the problems that exist?

Second, let's commit to a rational discussion based on facts, figures and findings, and avoid the hype and hysteria that only distorts the debate. If we do, we can calibrate policy reforms to avoid doing harm and deal with specific problems amenable to policy responses.

How do most immigrants enter the United States? Most immigrants enter the United States legally. The most common misconception in the immigration debate is that most enter illegally. According to a poll taken for *Time* magazine, when Americans were asked how most immigrants come into the United States, 64 percent answered "illegally," and 24 percent said "legally."

However, the Immigration and Naturalization Service reports that in fiscal 1992, 810,000 refugees and immigrants were legally admitted from overseas, and that an estimated 300,000 entered illegally. Furthermore, the Immigration and Naturalization Service estimated in October 1992 that the total population of those in the country illegally was 3.2 million. The five states with the largest estimated numbers of undocumented immigrants are California (1.3 million); New York (485,000); Florida (345,000); Texas (320,000); and Illinois (170,000). A total of 31 states had fewer than 10,000 undocumented immigrants. What this means is:

- Eight of 11 newcomers to the United States each year enter legally.
- Those residing in the United States illegally represent 1.25 percent of the population.
- In California, where the debate is especially heated, the undocumented immigrants comprise 4 percent of the state population.
- To the extent there are impacts, these are concentrated in a handful of states.

Other facts defy stereotypes regarding illegal immigration into the United States. For example, the top three nationalities of undocumented immigrants in New York are Ecuadoran, Italian and Polish. In fact, on a national basis, Mexicans are the lead group, but only comprise 30 percent of the undocumented immigrant population. And nearly half of the 300,000 immigrants who settle in the United States illegally each year do not sneak across the U.S.-Mexico border. They arrive legally with tourist or student visas and remain beyond their expiration date.

Another common misconception is that one can distinguish legal and undocumented immigrants on sight. In fact, many undocumented immigrants live in "mixed" households, where some residents are legal and others are not. Many are on their way to becoming legalized; and many, like their legal counterparts, are here to reunite with families, find shelter from political, religious or ethnic violence at home, or to obtain a decent wage.

The Causes of Illegal Immigration

What causes illegal migration? People move in search of freedom, family and work. The causes of uncontrolled migration in-

volve economic disparities, underdevelopment, political up-
heavals, oppression, population pressures and environmental
destruction. On a personal level, most people migrate by choice.
They want to provide for their family, to seek freedom and opportunity, to reunite with family members and to give their children a brighter future. Others leave out of necessity. They leave
to escape the knock on the door in the middle of the night, to
flee the bombs and bullets of civil war, to get out from under
the grinding boot of oppression and tyranny. Migration, particularly across national boundaries, is not generally for the tired
and poor, but for the strong and courageous. Giving up the
known for the unknown is an option chosen by risk-takers. Not
surprisingly, most international migrants are young, and, contrary to popular belief, women make up nearly half of the population. Trends indicate the percentage of women on the move
will increase in the coming decade.

Not Here for a Handout

Proposition 187 supporters claim that illegal aliens are flooding
California in search of welfare, free health care, and education.
Nonetheless, there is no evidence that Hispanic immigrants—
legal or illegal—come to the United States looking for a handout.
Even before Proposition 187 passed, illegal aliens were ineligible
for welfare benefits, although any of their children born in the
United States may receive assistance. Contrary to the image of
Hispanic immigrants living off welfare, the vast majority of Hispanic immigrants work. Indeed, 86 percent of Mexican men over
16 years of age are in the labor force, compared with only 75 percent of non-Hispanic whites.

Linda Chavez, *Crisis*, February 1995.

Given world population growth and the prevalence of poverty
and political violence in the developing world, is the United
States destined to be overrun by illegal immigration?
Most international migrants stay within the less developed
world: According to a 1992 World Bank estimate, there are 100
million international migrants, which represents one out of 50
people on the globe. Of that total, about two-thirds reside in less
developed countries, with the rest settling or working in Western Europe, North America and Australia. On an annual basis,
the United States receives—counting those admitted legally as
well as those who enter illegally—about 1.1 million newcomers
(700,000 legal immigrants, 120,000 refugees, and about 300,000
undocumented immigrants). Even when one adds the 450,000

workers, trainees and their family members who are admitted for temporary employment each year, the United States receives no more than 1.5 percent of the world's international migrants each year.

Most people uprooted by war and persecution are displaced in their own countries; most refugees (those who cross international boundaries in search of safety) seek protection in developing countries. The United Nations' High Commissioner for Refugees estimates that almost 20 million are counted as refugees. Of the total refugee population, about 90 percent seek safety in developing countries. The United States resettles 120,000 refugees a year (the refugees are screened and accepted from outside the United States), and receives about 100,000 asylum applications a year (those who come to the United States and apply for refugee status once here). This means that while the United States has one of the world's most generous refugee resettlement programs, no more than 1 percent of the world's refugee population finds its way here each year.

Impacts of Immigration

What is the economic impact of legal and illegal immigration on the United States? The impact is generally positive. According to an impressive body of knowledge from across the ideological spectrum, both legal and undocumented immigrants help our country's economic growth. In the most comprehensive study to date, the U.S. Department of Labor reported in 1989 that immigrants increase aggregate demand by encouraging investment; keep some U.S. industries competitive by increasing returns to capital; increase aggregate employment through higher rates of self-employment; and increase wages and mobility opportunities for many groups of U.S. workers. The same report notes that in cities with many immigrants, U.S. natives have not experienced widespread job displacement. Those who most directly feel the impact of job competition and wage pressures are earlier groups of immigrants.

What is the impact of illegal immigration on government services, costs and revenues? Undocumented immigrants work hard and use few government services. First, there are few federally funded public services that undocumented immigrants are eligible for. They include public school education from K–12; emergency Medicaid services; nutritional assistance to women, infants and children; and school lunch and breakfast. These services are available because the government has recognized that the social and economic costs of not providing them are likely to exceed the actual costs of providing the benefits.

The most concrete evidence of what social services undocumented immigrants do and do not use is based on Immigration and Naturalization Service surveys of immigrants who were legalized during the Amnesty Program of 1987–1988. At the time of application, less than 1 percent of the legalized immigrant population received general assistance, Social Security, Supplemental Security Income, workers compensation and unemployment insurance payments. Less than half of 1 percent obtained food stamps and Aid to Families with Dependent Children.

Moreover, before legalization, undocumented immigrants survived the old-fashioned way: They worked. Prior to being legalized, 83 percent participated in the labor force, which is 5 percent higher than the general population. Men worked on the average two hours a day more than men in the general population. Undocumented women worked five hours a day more than women in the general population.

A Nonexistent Problem

Nevertheless, in 1986 Congress mandated that the federal government introduce the Systematic Alien Verification for Entitlement (SAVE) system to keep undocumented immigrants from using Aid to Families with Dependent Children, Medicaid and food stamp programs. A 1992 audit conducted by the Agriculture Department's Office of Inspector General on the food stamp program concluded that "State agency officials agreed that the SAVE system was required for a nonexistent problem because their experience has been that undocumented aliens do not risk detection by applying for (food stamp) benefits. . . . We were able to identify only one case in a California (food stamp) county office where the SAVE system identified an illegal alien who applied for (food stamp) benefits."

As a result of the fact that undocumented immigrants work to survive and use few government services, it is estimated that they pay more money in taxes than they receive in social services. Professor Julian Simon of the University of Maryland, author of *The Economic Consequences of Immigration,* said undocumented immigrants pay five to 10 times more in taxes than the costs of services they use.

Pleading for Help

If the impacts are generally positive, why are state and local governments pleading with the federal government for help? The federal government receives most of the taxes paid by immigrants and shifts most of the costs to state and local governments. It is estimated that about two-thirds of the tax dollars paid by immigrants—legal and undocumented—go to the federal treasury, while most of the health, education and social service costs that are incurred are paid for by state and local governments, according to 1993 testimony by Charles Wheeler of the National

Immigration Law Center before the U.S. House Subcommittee on Human Resources. That's because most of those services are funded at the state and local level.

To add insult to injury, since 1982 the federal government has curtailed funding of programs that assist immigrants. For instance, refugee resettlement assistance was reduced from 36 months to eight months, while the federal contribution to refugees' receipt of state categorical aid was eliminated, according to Wheeler's testimony. Total federal expenditures dropped from more than $6,000 per refugee in 1982 to roughly $1,000 per refugee in 1993. Title VI Bilingual Education experienced a 47 percent decline in real expenditures between 1980 and 1991. This occurred at a time when from 1985 to 1990 the number of students who were considered "limited English proficient" was rising by 52 percent.

The Wrong Approach

What are the implications of these facts, figures and findings? First, it is clear that illegal immigration has become a victim of cheap politics rather than a challenge to practice good government. Instead of looking to objective evidence, some politicians and anti-immigrant groups cite bogus studies and exaggerated statistics to blame a small proportion of the population for complex problems of economic uncertainty and budget deficits.

This is not to suggest we should ignore the problem of illegal immigration. To the contrary, I believe it is the duty of sovereign nations to regulate who enters their territory and uphold the rule of law. I also believe we have an obligation to enforce our laws in a humane fashion consistent with democratic standards. For example, I support carefully conceived enforcement policies directed at deterring people at border crossings and airports as long as the enforcement officials respect human rights and are held accountable for the way they treat applicants for admission. On the other hand, I disfavor enforcement policies that target undocumented immigrants already residing in the country. Attempts to root people out of the work force, schools, health clinics and neighborhoods by introducing national identification cards, denying basic services and carrying out raids do more to discriminate against legal residents who look or sound "foreign," terrorize undocumented immigrants, and shift costs to state and local governments, than they do to reduce illegal immigration.

The time has come for the federal government to acknowledge the short-term costs related to immigration, which are borne primarily by state and local governments. While newcomers pay proportionally more in taxes than they receive in services, those taxes are primarily federal; state and local governments do not benefit as much from immigrants' tax dollars. This is not merely an immigration issue, but an issue of federalism. The federal government makes the policies, and the state and local governments feel the impact.

The Right Solutions

The immediate solution is for the federal government to create a viable assistance program for areas that receive the majority of new arrivals—legal and not. Redistributing federal largesse that is now going to states without significant immigrant populations to those areas disproportionately impacted by new arrivals is an equitable and intelligent approach to deal with the real health, education and social service costs borne by state and local governments.

The ultimate solution is to examine the root causes of immigration. Policies that treat international migration as a domestic enforcement issue will fall short of achieving the goal of curtailing illegal immigration. Grappling with causes rather than symptoms is neither easy nor politically popular. Nevertheless, it is where the possibility of progress lies.

The questions we should focus on, then, include: How can migration pressures be reduced by dealing with the "push" factors of relative poverty and political oppression, rather than fooling ourselves that heavy-handed enforcement is a sufficient response? What is the relationship among overpopulation, environmental degradation, underdevelopment, political instability, civil strife and migration? What policies and initiatives—such as trade, aid, debt relief, conflict prevention and resolution, voluntary family planning, comprehensive community development and democratic institution-building—might be carefully integrated and targeted to give people hope, security and opportunity at home, thereby removing the need to migrate?

The approaches suggested above may not be as appealing as heated rhetoric, inflated promises and highly visible crackdowns. It most certainly is not policy by sound bite. But it will produce results over time. In doing so, we enable the United States to continue its noble tradition of accepting legal immigrants and refugees, curtail illegal immigration and assist state and local governments to deal with the challenges of welcoming newcomers. Let us hope that rationality and responsible stewardship prevails over the politics of division and cynical opportunism.

"Illegal immigrants [are] taking advantage of expensive, state-provided social services, particularly health care."

Illegal Immigrants Abuse Health Care Services

Gayle Hanson

The federal government and most states provide emergency health care to illegal immigrants. In the following viewpoint, Gayle Hanson highlights cases in which illegal immigrants have fraudulently received expensive health care. Hanson contends that health care fraud by illegal immigrants is a particularly acute problem in California, where such abuse may go undetected because of a lack of investigators and the quality of counterfeit documents. Hanson is the West Coast correspondent for *Insight*, a weekly newsmagazine.

As you read, consider the following questions:

1. How much is the annual cost of caring for illegal immigrants, according to the author?
2. According to Hanson, what did California's Baby Cal advertising campaign promote?
3. Why is it difficult to resolve Medi-Cal investigations, in Hanson's opinion?

An ambulance pulled up outside Sharp Memorial Hospital in San Diego on Sept. 4, 1991, with a 42-year-old Hispanic man named Hermillo Meave inside. Despite the fact that he was being transferred with a chronic heart problem from a hospital in Tijuana, Mexico, Meave gave the hospital a San Diego address and claimed he worked in the area as a gardener with his brother. Since he could produce a California identification card and a Medi-Cal number that entitled him to treatment under the California health care system, Meave was ruled eligible for admission by a hospital-based Medi-Cal worker—meaning that virtually all of his expenses would be paid by the state.

Meave immediately began an elaborate and extremely expensive course of treatment. The day after he was admitted, surgeons implanted a pump to keep his heart beating until a donor organ could be found. For five months, Meave waited on the floor of the transplant unit until a heart was secured for him. Despite the suspicions of Medi-Cal fraud investigators—who suspected that he was not, as he claimed, a U.S. resident—Meave's application for a heart transplant was approved and in February 1992 he received a new heart.

Then the truth came out. "What Mr. Meave did was construct an incredibly elaborate fraud," says Kathleen Moore, head of the multi-organ transplant center at Sharp. "He had everybody fooled. The process of doing an organ transplant is very difficult and during the long months that a patient can wait for a suitable organ, people become very close. Well, Mr. Meave fooled everybody. The reality of the situation is that Mr. Meave actually lived and worked in Tijuana. He should never have been approved for a transplant."

The bill for Meave's care: $1 million.

A Growing Problem

The case of Hermillo Meave is only one of the most dramatic in what investigators and state officials say is a growing problem: a booming population of illegal immigrants taking advantage of expensive, state-provided social services, particularly health care. And state officials who handle the problem aren't happy about the policy coming out of Washington.

"When a ship drops 200 illegal Chinese immigrants off the coast of New Jersey, it's front-page news across the country," says San Diego County Supervisor Brian Bilbray. "But the truth is, we have 2,000 illegals coming across our border every night and the federal government is doing nothing to halt the problem. Bill Clinton says he wants to see the bill for the cost. The fact is, the federal government is the biggest deadbeat dad in the nation when it comes to paying for this problem. But at the same time it has set up laws that literally act like a magnet in attracting an illegal population."

California Gov. Pete Wilson has joined the governors of Texas, Florida, New York, Illinois, New Jersey and Arizona to try to force the federal government to pay the $7.5 billion annual cost of caring for the illegal-alien population—a group that in many cases receives better benefits than American citizens.

To focus more attention on the problem, Wilson held a press conference in March 1994 at the U.S.-Mexico border to announce the appointment of three more Medi-Cal fraud investigators. "This is the busiest border crossing in the world," he said. "Tens of thousands of people cross here every day. And we've discovered that many are going to illegally take advantage of California's generous taxpayer-financed social services. These skyrocketing costs are unfairly depriving California's legal residents of services they need and deserve. That's why I've repeatedly urged the federal government to either repeal these mandates or pay the bill for their failed policy."

California Bears the Brunt

Nearly half of the $7.5 billion total is owed to California, where the cost for providing services to undocumented immigrants is tallied at $3.6 billion annually. That money goes for everything from elementary and secondary education to prison cells—but increasingly for federally mandated health care.

Since 1986, when Congress passed the Omnibus Budget Reconciliation Act requiring states to provide emergency medical and childbirth services to all illegal immigrants through Medicaid programs, the number of people taking advantage of California's free medical care has grown eighteenfold. In 1988, about $22 million was paid to provide services to 31,600 illegal immigrants in California. To receive services, immigrants need only to declare their intention to remain in the United States. And to declare residency, they need only to produce a utility bill or a driver's license. In 1994, estimates show nearly $400 million was spent on care for about 390,000 illegal aliens.

"The federal government must gain control of our borders and must prevent massive illegal immigration," said Wilson. "The federal government must reimburse state taxpayers for the costs of federal failure."

Immigrants' Newborns

California is home to more than 2 million illegal immigrants, more than half the nation's total. But even beyond the cost of caring for the immigrants themselves, California increasingly is bearing the burden of caring for the American-born children of such immigrants. In 1992, nearly 96,000 babies were born to undocumented women under Medi-Cal coverage. Today, the largest increase in the state welfare rolls is among the infant children of illegal aliens. In fact, 40 percent of all publicly funded births are to illegal immigrants. As American citizens, these children immediately are eligible for a vast array of public assistance that in most cases also benefits their mothers.

"We have women coming here and they only know how to say two things in English," says Sally Super, director of the maternity pavilion at Sharp Chula Vista Hospital. "They want a birth certificate and they want to know how to apply for the WIC [Women, Infants and Children] Program.

Coming Across the Border

Soon after David Sossaman began work as an investigator for the San Diego County welfare-fraud unit, he was told by a colleague that thousands of Mexican citizens were crossing into Southern California to collect U.S. welfare benefits. Disbelieving but curious, he drove to the Chula Vista welfare office about seven miles from the Mexican border and noticed that many of the cars in the parking lot bore Mexican license plates.

Fluent in Spanish, Sossaman talked with the owner of one car, who confirmed that his wife was inside applying for welfare using a fictitious San Diego address. His friends and relatives in Mexico were already drawing checks. It was easy, they'd boasted, because welfare caseworkers verified neither eligibility nor citizenship.

Randy Fitzgerald, *Reader's Digest*, June 1994.

"I had a woman come into the emergency room whose water broke while she was swimming across the border. She was very, very sick, and so was her baby. I can't even begin to tell you how much it cost to take care of them. I believe that there are organized rings across the border that help these women get to California. Sometimes they'll come several months beforehand in order to set up house. And other times, they'll drive up here in Mercedes Benzes and Cadillacs and claim that they don't have jobs. But they know just what they are doing. They know just what to ask for."

Officials say that many of them are drawn by a program developed by the state of California that was designed to encourage undocumented pregnant women to seek prenatal care. In 1991, California launched a radio-television advertising campaign, dubbed Baby Cal, the goal of which was to promote good prenatal care for poor women statewide. From 1992 to 1994, however, nearly $80,000 has been spent on Spanish-language ads transmitted on Mexican radio and television stations. Such ads, say

95

critics, are nothing less than a magnet designed to encourage Mexican residents to come to the US. to have children.

"We aren't even allowed to ask them if they are here illegally," says Super. "It used to be that when they came here to have their babies they brought money. They were willing to pay something. Now, they don't bring anything. They know that the government will pay. I don't think that it is right for us to be providing health care for these people when we aren't doing the same thing for our own citizens. When I came here from South Dakota I was filled with compassion for them. But I have seen so much abuse of the system."

The Case of Rene Garcia

Indeed, the hills that rise up from the border between Mexico and Southern California are marked with trails that feed a steady supply of illegal immigrants. The border between Mexico and the United States is porous, and thousands legally cross it each day. They come to work, attend school and, in some cases, such as that of Rene Garcia, to commit fraud.

"It was New Year's Eve [1992] and we had an ambulance come to Sharp Chula Vista Hospital with a 24-year-old patient with a severe heart infection. He was with an uncle, who had a birth certificate and documentation showing that the patient's name was Rene A. Garcia and that he was an American citizen," recalls Marc Sandstrom. Sandstrom is senior vice president for legal and administrative services for Sharp Healthcare, a conglomerate that, through its hospitals and clinics, is the largest health care provider in San Diego County. "They put pressure on the hospital to do a heart transplant."

But at the Sharp Hospital oversight transplant center in San Diego, Moore recalls that they were unable to move ahead with the demand because Garcia had no insurance.

"The patient's uncle, Mr. Mario Cota, was asking us to go ahead and do the transplant and promising us that insurance would cover it, but we just aren't able to do things that way. Transplant procedures are extremely costly, both up front and in the long term, and we need to know that the patient has the financial ability to pay for that care," says Moore. "But Mr. Cota didn't understand that. He truly thought that just because Rene Garcia had papers saying he was an American citizen he would be entitled to have a heart transplant."

Incensed that the hospital did not move swiftly to perform the transplant, as it had done for Hermillo Meave, Cota took Rene Garcia's case to the Legal Aid Society of San Diego, where before the Board of Supervisors, a zealous attorney castigated the Medi-Cal investigators for needlessly jeopardizing Garcia's life. However, when the application for Medi-Cal was processed for

Rene A. Garcia, it turned out that nine other individuals were using the same documentation and that some of them had criminal records.

The Deception Ends

"It's funny, but when I first met the uncle I kept thinking that he was acting more like a father," recalls Medi-Cal fraud investigator Mark Miranda, who exposed the fraud. "And, in fact, that's who he turned out to be."

The patient, Rene Garcia, actually was a 24-year-old Mexican national named Jesus Ernesto Cota, whose father Mario Cota and uncle Marco Cota set up an elaborate masquerade in an attempt to finagle a free heart transplant. However, the deception ended bitterly in early March 1993 when the father was arrested on charges of attempted fraud. Three days after his father was jailed, Jesus Ernesto Cota died after being transferred to Sharp Memorial Hospital, leaving behind a medical bill of $200,000. The father, Mario Cota, has since pleaded guilty to the charges of fraud.

A family member, who asked to remain anonymous, said the middle-class family had spent more than $75,000 trying to obtain treatment for Jesus. At one time they had hoped to have the surgery performed in Mexico but were told the transplant was unlikely to occur because of the difficulty in getting suitable organs.

"I just wish that they would stop hounding us," said the family member. "But they just won't leave us alone. We did what we had to do."

So who will pick up the tab for Jesus Cota's hospitalization? The state has refused responsibility for the bill, leaving it up to the hospital to sue in hopes of recovering the costs.

"We don't want to be investigators," says Moore. "That should not have to be our job. We understand that this is a very emotional issue, but determining whether a person is who they say they are should not be the responsibility of the health care provider. We were lucky that our intake worker was suspicious."

Fraud Investigations

In response to the growing problem of Medi-Cal fraud, Wilson has beefed up the number of investigators from 66 to 101. But investigator Mark Miranda, who has been working out of San Diego since 1987, says that the scope of the problem is so large that it is likely that 50 percent more Medi-Cal applications could slip past the initial intake workers and ultimately prove to be fraudulent. Miranda faces each day with a thick stack of referrals for investigation—investigations that sometimes can turn dangerous.

"I've had people come after me with baseball bats, knives and broken bottles," he says. "I used to work in welfare investigation, and we weren't armed. But in this job they issue us a .38 special. I carry a 9mm Glock though, because I like the comfort of knowing that I have extra rounds of ammunition. In this job, you have to be prepared for everything."

The referrals Miranda receives are prepared by intake workers at local hospitals, doctors' offices or welfare centers. They usually end up on the desks of the fraud investigators when applications appear suspicious. Sometimes an individual will claim to have lived in the United States for five years and to be renting an apartment, but the person will have no job. Sometimes applicants have no identification. And sometimes too many will be shown applying from a single address. Miranda often clocks 1,500 miles a week on his car trying to track down fraud perpetrators from San Diego to the border.

"Here's an interesting one," he says, thumbing through a stack of about 75 referrals. "We have a 76-year-old woman whose husband is a policeman in Tijuana and who is eligible for Mexican health care. But it says on this referral that she claims that she has been living in the U.S. for the past six years with her daughter. Let's check this one out."

A Solid Lead

As Miranda drives through the gang-ridden southeastern section of the city, he spots a Tijuana license plate. "We should probably just follow that car," he quips. "I bet it'll take us right where we are going."

What Miranda intended as a casual joke turns into an accurate lead. As he pulls the state-issued Dodge into a parking place next to the car from Mexico, Miranda outlines the procedure he'll follow during the investigation. "When I go to a house, what I hope is that they can convince me that the person actually lives there and is who they say he is. You look for clothes in the closets, mail and any other indications that shows that the person is telling the truth."

Miranda knocks on the apartment's door and an older man answers. In fluent Spanish, Miranda introduces himself and explains that he is investigating on behalf of the health department Marguerite Reyes's application for Medi-Cal. Inside the apartment, Reyes, an elderly gray-haired woman, is introduced to Miranda. Throughout the visit she sits in a chair, her hands braced on a walker while she watches a Spanish-language variety show on television. Several other adults—who identify themselves as Reyes's daughter, son-in-law and son—mill in the background.

A birth certificate shows that Reyes was born in Texas. Suspicious, Miranda asks if he can have a look at her room, where he flips up the mattress. "This is always the first place I look," he says. "Nine times out of 10, people will keep things between their mattress and the box spring." There are letters, photos and bills, but Miranda has yet to find satisfactory documentation. Finishing up the investigation, his suspicions are still intact. But as he strolls towards his car, Reyes's son calls out in Spanish for him to return. "Ah," Miranda sighs. "It seems now they say they want to tell us the truth."

But the truth is still elusive. Reyes and her son launch into an elaborate explanation in which Reyes claims that her younger sister stole all of her identification and may in fact be using it to collect Medi-Cal or welfare benefits under Reyes's name.

"Well, this is going to take some looking into," Miranda admits as he leaves the apartment. "Sometimes these things resolve themselves in one visit. Not this one."

Difficult Cases

In the world along the border, it is not uncommon for people to have no birth certificate, no Social Security number, no identification at all. That makes some cases almost impossible to resolve. Miranda's next visit is to Ophelia Renteria, a woman who applied for Medi-Cal for her 6-year-old son Zury after he was hit by an automobile. Renteria's application was questioned when a hospital intake worker noticed that nine people were said to live in the two-bedroom apartment she gave as her address. But as Miranda discovers, she was telling the truth: Renteria, her husband and two children live in one of the bedrooms, her mother-in-law and her two children live in another bedroom and her brother and sister-in-law live in the living room. The apartment reeks of urine and the front yard is little more than a mud patch. Two blocks away a crack house is doing a brisk mid-afternoon business, as money and packages change hands at a busy intersection. Renteria has no identification—so, is her child entitled to Medi-Cal?

"Well, she says that she has applied for amnesty," says Miranda. "Her other child was born in the U.S. so is a citizen. And it looks like Zury probably qualifies for Medi-Cal coverage as [Renteria] says she has been here for five years."

What irks many people about the policy, from nurses providing maternity care to social workers involved in qualifying recipients, is that many of the services provided to undocumented immigrants simply are not available to legal residents.

"People across the country don't realize the magnitude of the problem," says Sandra Smoley, California's secretary of health and welfare. "But the truth of the matter is that these are federal policies that are being supported by taxpayer money. When we first met with the Clinton people, we felt that they understood the severity of the problem. But they have done nothing about it. Certainly with [White House chief of staff] Leon Panetta being from California we had hoped that they would be more supportive.

"In California this is seen as a taxpayer issue, and we have bipartisan support to do something about it. But when five states are bearing the overwhelming burden of the problem it is hard for people to realize, unless they come here, just how serious things are. In February 1994, we put an investigator at the border crossing at San Ysidro to check documentation of people crossing. We believe he has already saved the state about $400,000. So we're adding investigators at both the Tecate and Otay crossings," she adds.

Pressure on Washington

Wilson has pressured Washington to address the mounting problem. Already there have been talks of a lawsuit against the federal government to force changes in the law. Wilson also wants to see a constitutional amendment denying the rights of citizenship to children of illegal aliens. However, it is unlikely that the political will exists to push such changes through.

"Frankly, we're still just sticking our fingers in the dike," says Wilson. "The real solution to this problem is for the federal government to control the border, pay the bill and repeal the mandates. That's the real answer to this problem."

In the meantime, emergency rooms will still be overwhelmed, social workers' resources will be stretched and investigators such as Miranda will plug away at a problem that he candidly acknowledges could be even larger than what already is documented.

"It's hard to know how many cases just slip through," says Miranda. "On the cases that we do have referred, a high percentage of them are fraudulent. As for the ones that we never see, let's say they could be another 25 to 50 percent."

"Many injuries and health problems suffered by the undocumented in the United States go unreported based on the victim's fear of detection and deportation."

Illegal Immigrants Do Not Abuse Health Care Services

Antonio R. Velasco

In the following viewpoint, Antonio R. Velasco argues that rather than abusing health care services, illegal immigrants are being excluded from the health care system and that, consequently, their serious health care problems are not being addressed. Velasco maintains that many undocumented workers, in particular California's large population of farmworkers, are plagued by health problems due to malnutrition, unsanitary living conditions, and lack of health insurance. Velasco is a family practitioner in Salinas, California, and an associate professor of family medicine at the University of California at San Francisco School of Medicine.

As you read, consider the following questions:

1. What is the average life expectancy of Latino farmworkers, according to Velasco?
2. In Velasco's opinion, how many Salvadorans fled national strife for the United States?
3. What is the average waiting period for prenatal care in Los Angeles County, according to the author?

Abridged from Antonio R. Velasco's paper presented at The Undocumented Immigrant and the Health Care Crisis Forum on Immigration: Its Terms and Consequences, held at the Cross-Cultural Center of the University of California at Davis, March 11, 1994. Reprinted by permission of the author.

With the recent spotlight of public attention focused on a marginalized and impoverished sector of American society, the undocumented immigrant living in the United States today is clearly faced with many hardships.

Any discussion concerning the plight of undocumented workers must be viewed from the perspective and context of the entire Latino Community. For example, if Latinos, as a group, suffer more and are dying faster than other groups in this country, then it is even more a certainty for undocumented workers. For example, the average life expectancy of Latino farmworkers in the U.S. is 49 years, compared with a national average of 75 years for non-Latinos.

If Latinos represent 3.2 million, or 49.9 percent, of California's approximately 6.4 million uninsured, it can be assumed that the number of undocumented workers who are denied access to health care in this country is much greater. In recent years we've heard accounts about the lives of these undocumented immigrants, but what do we really know about them? Who are the undocumented immigrants? Where do they come from? And how can we separate facts from myths? How can we distinguish the rhetoric from the reality? News accounts provide a partial glimpse of this reality:

- Undocumented workers found living in caves.
- Undocumented immigrants drowned in canals and rivers.
- Immigrants discovered dying in locked box cars out in the desert.
- Undocumented immigrants hunted like animals; raped, robbed or assaulted by armed bandits and gangs along the border.

Perhaps a clearer indication of this population's quality of life can be found by evaluating the community's medical needs and the daily conditions in which they survive.

A Variety of Health Problems

In our Monterey County clinics and hospitals, we have treated undocumented immigrants for a variety of health problems, including poisonings form the daily exposure to pesticides. These are the very same insecticides that were originally designed in times of war to serve as chemical warfare agents, which are now used to protect our bountiful harvest and preserve our nation's billion-dollar-a-year agribusiness.

In agriculture, more than 900 million pounds of pesticides are applied yearly. Those having the highest contact with toxic materials, like farmworkers, face the greatest health risks.

In our practice we have also examined the babies born with low birth weights to undocumented mothers that were either too poor or too fearful to approach us for prenatal care. Babies born weighing under 5.5 pounds, often prematurely, represent the highest risk of infant mortality and morbidity within the Latino population. Low-birth-weight infants are known to have 40 times the risk of dying in the first month of life. Women are denied prenatal care, despite research showing that for every $1 spent on preventative prenatal care, $3 of the taxpayer's money is saved.

Patiently, and sometimes impatiently, we have listened to the disturbing arguments being promoted through the media and by politicians who assert that the presence of undocumented immigrants in the United States represents an unfair burden to society. They claim that jobs are being taken from more worthy and needy Americans, that undocumented immigrants exhaust our limited resources and, in general, seriously threaten the American way of life. Yet, despite all of this, despite these arguments, little evidence has surfaced to support these claims.

Economics and the Undocumented

On the contrary, multiple studies have clearly shown that undocumented workers contribute much more to society than they extract. By the very nature of being undocumented, this primarily Latino population is greatly understudied and unquestionably underserved.

Research indicates that most undocumented immigrants come from Mexico and parts of Central America. Today, nine of every ten farmworkers in California are foreign-born, mostly from Mexico. Exact numbers of undocumented immigrants in California range from as little as 70,000 to more than 1.3 million. This number, according to government officials, may be increasing by as many as 100,000 annually.

In 1994, 28 percent, or one out of every four Latino workers had a family income below the poverty level, compared to 9 percent for Anglo workers.

Today in California there are as many as 881,000 farmworkers, according to the California Department of Employment Development. Most workers tend to be young. Three out of four are men, two out of three are married, 55 percent have been in the United States fewer than nine years and one in every five workers admits to being undocumented. The median total family income of migrant farmworkers in the United States, according to a 1990 report by the National Migrant Resource Program, fell below the poverty level at $9,000 for a family of four, compared to the $11,000 national poverty threshold.

War in El Salvador

Armed conflicts, civil unrest, extreme poverty in Latin America, combined with the basic human need to pursue a better life can account for the sizable increase in undocumented immigration to the United States.

In El Salvador, for example, the 12 years of brutal civil war claimed more than 75,000, mostly civilian lives, and forced unprecedented levels of internal and external displacement. During the Reagan and Bush administrations of the 1980s, the United States sent more than $6 billion in military and economic assistance to support the Salvadoran government.

In the U.S.-backed war against leftist insurgents, as many as 1.5 million Salvadorans fled the violence and entered the United States illegally. Only 1.3 percent of these Salvadorans were ever granted political asylum during the war. The remaining 98.7 percent who were not granted political asylum faced the ultimate risk of being deported back to El Salvador: almost certain death by execution.

No Freeloaders

It is said that illegal immigrants take jobs away from American citizens. It is also said that they place a drain on the already strained California educational system and medical resources. I can't argue with these points. But I can say that [two of] the illegal aliens I encountered [as a Los Angeles County surgeon] hurt their hands on the job, working vigorously to earn a living.

They did not seek tax-subsidized medical attention after a barroom brawl or a drunken wall-punching incident. I have no data to support this, but I would bet that the money the state and county spent to treat their hand injuries was more than returned to the California economy in the form of productivity from these men.

Lloyd M. Krieger, *New York Times*, August 28, 1995.

According to the United Nations, rural poverty, high fertility and environmental degradation are the driving forces behind the mass increase in immigration throughout the world today.

In 1992, state records show that $1.7 billion was spent for education, medical needs and law enforcement for undocumented people. From 1975 to 1992, the INS [Immigration and Naturalization Service] tripled its budget and doubled its staff, all in an effort to curb undocumented immigration.

At the same time, it is impossible to calculate the economic benefits gained by the labor of undocumented immigrants in this country over the past decades. Undocumented immigrants, as an expendable, cheap source of labor, pay out millions of dollars a year in Social Security and other taxes that they are not eligible to ever collect on.

The Plight of the Undocumented Workers

A review of undocumented worker abuses and violations includes the exploitation of child labor; minimum-wage violations; lack of worker's compensation insurance; unregulated farm-labor contractors; overpriced, overcrowded and unhealthy housing conditions; the lack of health benefits; limited or no access to basic primary medical care; the threat of infectious diseases, including tuberculosis and AIDS; parasites; nutritional problems; and occupational hazards. All of this under the constant fear of detection, discrimination, persecution and deportation.

Undocumented immigrant health care in general is impossible to consider without emphasizing the dramatic and marginalized conditions in which they live.

By definition, undocumented immigrants are poor. Many enter the United States seeking to break the cycle of poverty they come from, only to find further hardships here. Those that find menial employment, mostly in manual labor, are often obligated to support not only their immediate family here, but families outside of the United States. These added financial burdens further jeopardize the health and well-being of the undocumented immigrants while living in the United States.

Still people keep coming. In 1992, government studies show that more than 1.2 million undocumented immigrants attempted to enter the United States illegally. Of this number, 370,000 were deported.

Housing Conditions

Overall, housing conditions for undocumented immigrants are inadequate and at times nonexistent. As recently as 1992, near Salinas, as many as 700 undocumented immigrant farmworkers were found living in caves and make-shift shelters.

Some of the workers had obtained their drinking water from the pesticide-laden irrigation system. Migrant farm work is transient and seasonal in nature, making housing demands competitive and difficult to obtain for many undocumented newcomers. Those who find housing in migrant worker camps pay as much as $500 a month for a two-bedroom apartment, while earning as little as $4.25 an hour.

In addition, from 1984 to 1994, employer-provided housing for workers has decreased by 75 percent. The lack of sanitary facilities and the unsanitary, substandard housing contribute to the spread of communicable diseases.

Occupational Health Problems

Pesticide poisoning represents one of the gravest threats to undocumented immigrant health in this country.

Farmwork-related deaths are the highest for all occupations in the United States. In a 1987 study, agricultural workers led the field with 49 work-related deaths per 100,000, followed by 38 deaths per 100,000 for miners and 35 deaths per 100,000 for construction workers.

According to 1992 studies conducted by the Department of Medicine at the University of California, Davis, potential farmwork-related health problems include accidents, pesticide-related illnesses, musculoskeletal and soft tissue disorders, dermatitis, noninfectious respiratory conditions, reproductive health problems, communicable diseases, bladder and kidney disorders, diabetes, hypertension and children's health problems.

Again, considering the lack of documentation and specific data pertaining to the status of undocumented immigrant health in this country, we still can conclude that all of the above mentioned problems also seriously impact the population. Many injuries and health problems suffered by the undocumented in the United States go unreported based on the victim's fear of deportation.

Including the undocumented population among the rank and file of migrant farm work may give us a fair indication of the status of this crisis. In 1987, for example, 25 percent of all reported pesticide-related illnesses were in agricultural workers. Underreporting of pesticide poisoning is common and it is estimated that less than 2 percent of all incidents are ever documented.

The discovery of childhood cancer clusters in two small communities surrounded by grapes, a very intensive pesticide-use crop, raises the issue of cancer risk to children and other farmworkers.

Two other factors that affect the reporting and health care of undocumented immigrants with pesticide-related illnesses are that many people fail to recognize the symptoms of poisoning. Along with this, pesticide cases are sometimes handled improperly by doctors sympathetic to the agri-industry who cover up incidents or fail to diagnose the problem properly.

The health of the undocumented immigrant who works in agriculture is seriously threatened by the high levels of alcohol and drug abuse that is found in the farmworker population. Studies show that substance abuse is a major problem among farmworkers, particularly those who work in lettuce harvest. The harsh demands of field work and the lifestyle of the mostly young male undocumented immigrant in the United States make drug use common, including cocaine, marijuana and heroin.

Infectious Diseases

The incidence of tuberculosis [TB] and AIDS in the undocumented immigrant population has been increasing for some time in the United States. Undocumented immigrants also encounter serious health risks through sexually transmitted dis-

106

ease, such as gonorrhea, herpes, syphilis and chlamydia.

Again, since the majority of the undocumented immigrants in the United States are young males, many do not consider the health risks involved in unsafe sexual practices while living away from families and wives left behind in their home countries. At the same time, Latina women, both in the United States and those remaining behind, but still having contact with their partners during visits, are exposed to these dangerous diseases.

Latinas have the highest incidence (3.5 per 100,000) of heterosexually acquired AIDS of any male or female ethnic group in the United States. As a group, Latinos, with only 9 percent of the total population in the United States, comprise 16 percent of all reported cases of AIDS. In 1991, for example, the incidence of AIDS in the U.S. was 31.6 per 100,000 population among Latinos and 11.8 per 100,000 among non-Latinos.

From 1989 to 1990, Latinos also showed a larger proportionate increase (13.5 percent) in AIDS cases than any other racial or ethnic group. By 1988, in the Northeastern United States AIDS was the leading cause of death in Latino and African American children under the age of four. In 1991, the rates for AIDS cases among Latinos (adults and children) were 2.5 to 7.5 times higher than rates for comparable groups of non-Latinos.

Overcrowding and a nomadic lifestyle leave migrant workers especially vulnerable to contracting tuberculosis. Migrant farmworkers, often recruited from labor camps and homeless shelters throughout the country by independent farm labor contractors, are exposed to the disease. From 1984 to 1990, the incidence of TB has increased by 16 percent (25,700 cases in 1990—up from 22,000 in 1984).

Many farmworkers come from areas in which TB is endemic. The difficulty in establishing the diagnosis and the prolonged nature of the treatment can become impossible obstacles to overcome in eradicating this disease. Also, due to the manner of transmission (airborne particle) epidemics are likely to result when a few individuals are left untreated.

Mortality and Malnutrition

According to a November 1993 study in the *Journal of the American Medical Association*, the mortality rate of Latinos in the United States is influenced by cultural, social and economic factors. "Hispanic populations have a greater proportion of persons living in poverty and a greater proportion without health insurance than do non-Hispanic whites," the report stated. Latinas are three times less likely to receive prenatal care than non-Latinas. Those without prenatal care are twice as likely to deliver low-birth-weight infants, who in turn, are 40 times more likely to die in the first month of life.

Access to family planning and abortion is also a health issue and is influenced by cultural, religious, social and economic factors.

Given the poor living conditions, low wages and dangerous occupations, undocumented immigrants that toil in our country's field are also likely to go hungry. In order to save money, undocumented immigrants often skimp on food or do not earn enough to feed both themselves and their families properly.

In a 1990 issue of *Public Health Reports*, a dietary assessment study of Latino migrant farmworkers in North Carolina revealed 84 percent of the women had dietary recalls showing caloric intakes at less than 90 percent of their RDA [recommended dietary allowance]. The survey further showed that of this same population only one-third of the infants and children received 90 percent or more of the RDA for calories.

Anemia among farmworker children is common. A health study found that in some poor communities 71 percent of Latino children needed medical referral. One-quarter of the children were experiencing anemia as a result of malnutrition, and fully one-half had never been to a dentist, even for an examination, the study showed. These conditions predispose people to other illnesses and can certainly decrease their life expectancy.

While California's overall infant mortality rate improved between 1980 and 1990, the rate in the Latino community has deteriorated. Stillbirths among Latinos increased by 45 percent between 1987 and 1989 while during the same time period the infant and fetal death rate in Los Angeles County also rose. Causes for increases in infant mortality can be attributed to poor nutrition, smoking and drug use among the Latino population. Still, the greatest risk factor to newborns involved the lack of prenatal care.

The average waiting period to obtain a prenatal appointment in a Los Angeles County clinic is more than 16 weeks. By the time a patient can see a doctor, the critical first trimester of pregnancy is over.

Health Insurance and Health Care Barriers

Of the more than 6 million Californians that do not have health insurance, 3 million are Latino. Needless to say, given the percentages, undocumented immigrants in California are twice as likely not to have health insurance as documented Latinos.

Long waits in doctor's offices, language barriers, low education levels of immigrants, high medical costs, fear of detection, and travel time from remote communities to receive preventative and primary care are all influential factors in the lack of quality care to this country's undocumented population. In California, the costs for health insurance in 1989 for a family of four ranged from between $2,500 to $4,000 annually. Given this amount it seems highly unlikely that undocumented immigrants would spend between one-third and one-half of their annual income on health insurance.

In 1991, the U.S. spent over $700 billion on personal health care services. Twenty-five percent of this sum was spent on administrative costs to insurance companies. There are presently 37 million uninsured Americans in the country and this figure is expected to rise. . . .

Perhaps as many as 1.3 million undocumented immigrants in the State of California will continue to be excluded from access to health care. As they are not eligible for government and state medical benefits, they will continue to present themselves at hospital emergency rooms throughout the state in acute need. At the last minute, oftentimes while in critical condition, they will present themselves to hospital personnel who have no knowledge of their personal or medical history. We know from experience that patients without insurance are 140 percent more likely to die of the same illness than an insured patient.

This scenario, which occurs all too often, is far too expensive on an already overburdened health care system and is far too risky for both the patient and the health care provider. Whatever decisions are made affecting the status of health care reform in the United States, it appears clear that undocumented immigrants will remain a stigmatized and forgotten sector of American society.

Periodical Bibliography

The following articles have been selected to supplement the diverse views presented in this chapter. Addresses are provided for periodicals not indexed in the *Readers' Guide to Periodical Literature*, the *Alternative Press Index*, or the *Social Sciences Index*.

Trevor Armbrister	"Our Drug-Plagued Mexican Border," *Reader's Digest*, January 1996.
David Beacon	"Putting L.A. on the Map: How California's Immigrant Workers Are Revitalizing Labor," *Village Voice*, March 19, 1996. Available from 36 Cooper Square, New York, NY 10003.
William Branigin	"Conning Their Way into the Country," *Washington Post National Weekly Edition*, December 11–17, 1995. Available from Reprints, 1150 15th St. NW, Washington, DC 20071.
G. Russell Evans	"The Crisis of Illegal Immigration," *Conservative Review*, March/April 1994. Available from 1307 Dolley Madison Blvd., Rm. 203, McLean, VA 22101.
Randy Fitzgerald	"Welfare for Illegal Aliens?" *Reader's Digest*, June 1994.
Michael Fix and Jeffrey S. Passel	"Who's on the Dole? It's Not Illegal Immigrants," *Los Angeles Times*, August 3, 1994. Available from Reprints, Times Mirror Square, Los Angeles, CA 90053.
William P. Hoar	"The Importation of Crime," *New American*, April 4, 1994. Available from 770 Westhill Blvd., Appleton, WI 54914.
Lloyd M. Krieger	"Illegal Aliens, Dirty Jobs," *Los Angeles Times*, August 28, 1995.
Howard LaFranchi	"Drugs Surge from Mexico as U.S. Hunts for Solution," *Christian Science Monitor*, February 29, 1996. Available from Reprints, 1 Norway St., Boston, MA 02115.
John Martin	"Immigration as a National Security Issue," *Immigration Review*, Winter 1995. Available from Center for Immigration Studies, 1815 H St. NW, Washington, DC 20006.
Charley Reese	"Preserve America or Lose It," *Conservative Chronicle*, April 12, 1995. Available from PO Box 11297, Des Moines, IA 50340-1297.
Richard Rothstein	"Immigration Dilemmas," *Dissent*, Fall 1993.
John Tanton and Wayne Lutton	"Welfare Costs for Immigrants," *Social Contract*, Fall 1992. Available from 316½ E. Mitchell St., Petoskey, MI 49770.

How Should America Respond to Illegal Immigration?

Chapter Preface

In February 1995, Bill Clinton outlined America's strongest-ever strategy to secure the U.S.-Mexico border. The plan included increased funding for the deployment of thousands more Border Patrol agents and high-tech equipment to monitor the border. U.S. Border Patrol funding for equipment such as ground sensors, high-intensity lighting, and night-vision cameras more than doubled from 1994 ($124 million) to 1996 ($295 million). Additionally, in October 1995, U.S. attorney general Janet Reno appointed America's first "border czar" to coordinate illegal-immigration control at the southwest border.

According to California congressman Duncan Hunter, Border Patrol agents along the U.S.-Mexico border should number "about 10,000 agents, so that every several hundred yards you have a couple of Border Patrol agents on a twenty-four-hour basis." Whether or not that many agents are eventually assigned, Immigration and Naturalization Service commissioner Doris Meissner contends, "The [border strategy] works. With a variety of tactics, we are stopping the revolving door of illegal immigration."

But some activists and officials contend that this policy is ineffective because it does not address the demand for undocumented workers. According to California assistant labor commissioner Jose Millan, as long as employers need undocumented workers, "they can put cops shoulder to shoulder and they'll come in by boat or plane or some other way." Others warn that the southwest border is becoming too militarized, patrolled by increasing numbers of state National Guards and U.S. soldiers. In the words of San Diego immigration rights activist Roberto Martinez, the growing armed presence along the border is "a low-intensity warfare against immigrants. The Border Patrol is already armed to the teeth."

Fortifying the U.S.-Mexico border is one of a variety of responses to illegal immigration that are debated throughout this chapter.

"The cost of ignoring the real and explosively growing problem of illegal immigration is far greater than the cost of fixing it."

America Should Bar All Illegal Immigrants

Pete Wilson

Pete Wilson is the governor of California. In 1994, he initiated lawsuits against the federal government for the reimbursement of state costs incurred from illegal immigration. In the following viewpoint, Wilson argues that illegal immigrants should be barred and deported from California and the United States. He contends that the federal government must adopt stricter policies against illegal immigrants, including stronger enforcement of immigration laws and quicker deportation of criminal aliens.

As you read, consider the following questions:

1. How much do illegal immigrants cost California taxpayers, according to the author?
2. Whom does Wilson blame for the federal government's failure to reimburse states?
3. What does Wilson encourage California cities and counties to do regarding the costs of illegal immigrants?

Pete Wilson, "Securing Our Nation's Borders," a speech delivered at the Los Angeles Townhall, April 25, 1994, and reprinted in *Vital Speeches of the Day*, November 15, 1994. Reprinted by permission of the author.

I filed suit against the federal government for its failure to control our nation's borders. It's not a decision I came to lightly. I would rather resolve this crisis in the Congress than in the courts. But the repeated failure of Congress to confront its responsibility to control illegal immigration and to prevent the terrible unfairness to state taxpayers and to needy legal residents—has driven us to seek redress for our injuries in the courts.

The federal government's immigration policy is broken and the time to fix it is now.

It's hard to blame people who day after day pour across our borders. They're coming to find a better life for themselves and their families. It's easy to sympathize with them and even admire their gumption. It is those in Washington that we should condemn—those who encourage the illegals to break the law by rewarding them for their illegal entry.

We are a state and a nation of immigrants, proud of our immigrant traditions. Like many of you, I'm the grandchild of immigrants. My grandmother came to this country in steerage from Ireland at age 16. She came for the same reason any immigrant comes—for a better future than she could hope for in the old country. And America benefited from her and millions like her.

But we, as a sovereign nation, have a right and an obligation to determine how and when people come into our country. We are a nation of laws, and people who seek to be a part of this great nation must do so according to the law.

A Limit to Generosity

The United States already accepts more legal immigrants into our country than the rest of the world combined—1.8 million in 1991 alone. We are a generous people. But there is a limit to what we can absorb and illegal immigration is now taxing us past that limit.

Thousands come here illegally every day. In fact, the gaping holes in federal policy have made our borders a sieve. President Bill Clinton has used that very word to describe their porous condition.

The results are, in Los Angeles, there's now a community of illegal residents numbering a million people. That's a city the size of San Diego. Alone, it would be the seventh largest city in the nation—half again the population of our nation's capital, Washington, D.C. Two-thirds of all babies born in Los Angeles public hospitals are born to illegal immigrants. As we struggle to keep dangerous criminals off our streets, we find that 14 percent of California's prison population are illegal immigrants—enough to fill 8 state prisons to design-capacity.

And through a recession that has caused the loss of one-third the revenues previously received by state government, as we have struggled to maintain per pupil spending and to cover fully enrollment growth with classrooms around the state bursting at the seams, we're forced to spend $1.7 billion each year to educate students who are acknowledged to be in the country illegally.

In total, California taxpayers are compelled *by federal law* to spend more than $3 billion to provide services to illegal immigrants—it's approaching 10 percent of our state budget.

Reason and Responsibility

To ignore this crisis of illegal immigration—as some would have us do—is not only irresponsible, but makes a mockery of our laws. It is a slap in the face to the tens of thousands who play by the rules and endure the arduous process of legally immigrating to our country. It's time to restore reason, integrity and fairness to our nation's immigration policy. And we need to do it now. California can't afford to wait.

First, the federal government must secure our border. That's the first step in securing our future. They must devote the manpower and the technology necessary to prevent people from crossing the border in the first place.

Second, the federal government should turn off the magnetic lure that now rewards people who successfully evade the border patrol and cross the border illegally.

Back to Their Countries of Origin

The promise of a free education is only one of the magnets we have created to encourage people to violate our borders. It should be clear that any solution to our immigration crisis must include an elimination of these incentives. Allowing states to make their own decisions on [who is eligible for] education serves this purpose.

Illegal immigrants belong back in their countries of origin, and we should do everything possible to encourage them to embrace that simple truth.

Elton Gallegly, *Los Angeles Times*, April 4, 1995.

And finally, until our representatives in Washington do act, until they secure the border and turn off the magnetic lure, they should pay the full bill for illegal immigration. The states shouldn't be forced to bear the cost for a failed federal policy that gives a free pass to those who breach our borders, then passes the buck to us.

Those who oppose reform invariably cry racism. They want to stifle even any discussion of the issue.

But this debate isn't about race, it's about responsibility and resources. Washington must accept responsibility for this strictly federal issue, and California must be allowed to devote our limited resources to those people who have come to our country through the legal process. This isn't a partisan issue, or even simply a California issue. Washington's failure to bear responsibility for illegal immigration is forcing states around the nation to bear enormous costs.

And we have finally started to see some recognition of the problem in Washington. Working with our Congressional delegation on the Budget Resolution before Congress, we've secured the strongest Congressional statement yet for full reimbursement. It fully acknowledges federal responsibility for criminal aliens who have committed felonies under state law only because they were permitted to enter the country illegally by virtue of federal failure to control the border.

Quicker and Stronger Responses Are Needed

In the 1994 federal crime bill, the House of Representatives added amendments mandating federal incarceration of criminal aliens or reimbursements to states for the cost of their incarceration—but not until 1998! The official rationale for this four-year delay in the arrival of the cavalry is that Congress requires the time to find a way to pay. Meanwhile, the states are to continue patiently laying out what is proportionately a far greater share of our budgets for what is acknowledged to be an exclusively federal duty.

In April 1994, the Clinton Administration took a positive, but inadequate step towards reimbursing states for the costs of keeping alien felons locked up in state prisons. The $350 million authorized by the White House for all states is little more than half what is required according to the Congressional Budget Office estimate, and in fact is less than they owe California alone.

Another amendment to the crime bill authorizes the addition of 6,000 agents to the Border Patrol, but these House authorizations now must pass the Senate to take effect. And even then, they are just *authorizations*, just acknowledgments of the problem. Congress must then take the next step, *appropriation*—which means voting to actually cut a check to pay the costs imposed on the states by federal failure to control the borders and federal mandates to provide services to illegal immigrants.

And we've watched, time and time again, as Congress has authorized reimbursement in the spring, but then stripped out or failed to pass an appropriation, and left us holding the bag in the fall.

That's why we have launched an unprecedented offensive by a bipartisan coalition of seven states, including the five most populous, to pressure the Administration and Congress to do eq-

116

uity and honor the federal obligation to reimburse us. They should do so in the federal budget and appropriation bills.

Suing the Federal Government

But we will not stand by and watch the political process fail once again, when we can wait no longer. So, in addition to pursuing reform in Washington, we launched a series of lawsuits against the federal government. Unfortunately, Congress' track record of failure has compelled us to seek a remedy in the courts, even as we continue a bipartisan, multi-state effort to pressure the Administration and Congress to atone for and pay for their sins by corrective action both at the border and in the appropriation process.

In court, we'll seek two broad goals. First, that the federal government enforce our nation's immigration laws and secure our nation's border. And second, that the federal government reimburse California fully for costs incurred when it fails to enforce the law.

Suing for reimbursement is not only a matter of fairness for state taxpayers, it's a matter of making the political process work for our nation. Immigration and control of our nation's border are, by virtue of the Constitution, a strictly federal responsibility. But today, there is no fiscal accountability for that policy.

The Congress is writing blank checks on other people's bank accounts—and one of those accounts belongs to the taxpayers of California. Congress must be forced to bear the fiscal consequences for its immigration policy. If they have to pay the bill for that policy, if they feel the pinch in the federal budget for which they alone are accountable to the voters, then and only then will they have the incentive to fix this policy that simply doesn't work.

President Clinton has acknowledged as much himself. In 1993 he said, "One of the reasons the federal government has not been forced to confront this . . . is that the states of California, Texas and Florida have had to bear a huge portion of the costs for the failure of federal policy."

Do Not Ignore the Problem

It's a fundamental element of democracy—a government must be held accountable for its actions. And if the federal government were held accountable, they would quickly discover that the cost of ignoring the real and explosively growing problem of illegal immigration is far greater than the cost of fixing it.

They would see that the federal resources necessary to secure our nation's border are dwarfed by the billions that California and other states spend today in making massive illegal immigration to America a safety-net for the world. What's more, by compelling California to provide this safety-net for illegals, the feds are tearing gaping holes in the safety-net we seek to provide for our own needy legal residents.

For 1995, the Clinton Administration proposed increasing spending on border enforcement across the country by just $180 million a year. We'll spend nearly 10 times that amount just educating illegal immigrants in California schools.

In April 1994 I went to El Paso, where I saw firsthand a program known as Operation Hold the Line that has used a blockade to reduce illegal crossings by 75 percent. I will concede that the same plan that has produced such success for the El Paso Blockade can't be precisely reproduced everywhere on the border. But the most important lesson to draw from El Paso is that we *can* control our border.

Those who say the effort is futile . . . those who say we should simply concede that people who want to cross the border will . . . are wrong. But to secure our border, we first need a plan. Then we must devote the will and resources to carry it out, as they have in El Paso.

But the officials responsible in Washington fail to see the urgency of the problem. INS [Immigration and Naturalization Service] Commissioner Doris Meissner said, and I quote, "There's nothing wrong in taking a year or two [to enact immigration reform]."

Forcing Action

Well, Ms. Meissner, I don't know what border you're looking at, but as the people who bear the cost for your failed policy, we can tell you that two years is too long to wait. Every *day* we wait, the problem grows worse. That's why we're taking our case to court. Since we must, we will force the federal government to bear responsibility for its policies.

Our first lawsuit, filed in April 1994, seeks reimbursement for the costs California bears for incarcerating alien felons in our state prisons. The price tag in 1994 alone is nearly $400 million, and that doesn't include the costs from previous years, the capital costs for housing these criminals, or the costs to county governments.

But our suit will also seek to compel the federal government to do its duty to enforce immigration laws already on the books. Specifically, we'll demand that the federal government be forced to take custody of the thousands of alien felons who have completed their sentences in state prison, but are back on the street, because the INS has failed to deport them. That federal dereliction forces California to supervise parole for 4,400 criminal aliens every day.

We'll demand that the federal government begin prosecuting

118

alien felons who return to the U.S., currently a federal offense punishable by up to 15 years in prison, but one routinely ignored by federal officials.

And we will demand that federal officials be required to deport alien criminals to the interior of their home country and not continue the absurd practice of simply dumping them at the border, where all too often they simply re-enter the U.S. across the porous border and beat the bus back to L.A.

Additional suits will address other parts of the federal government's failed policy—a policy that has cost the taxpayers of California more than $10 billion in education, medical and prison costs for illegal immigrants since 1988.

And I'm encouraging the cities and counties of California to also file suit to seek reimbursement for the costs owed to them by the federal government.

Our goal, though, is larger than simply seeking reimbursement—as important and as urgently needed as it is. Our goal is to force the federal government to accept responsibility for the crisis of illegal immigration. Only when they accept responsibility will Congress finally adopt the reforms necessary to restore integrity and fairness to our immigration laws.

Once Congress is forced to confront this problem, I'm sure it will waste no time in doing what's necessary to secure our nation's borders. And securing our nation's borders is the only way we can secure the future we want for California.

"Americans must begin to accept the fact that free trade and open borders are to their utmost benefit."

America Should Admit All Immigrants

Thomas E. Lehman

In the following viewpoint, Thomas E. Lehman argues that it would be in America's best interest to open its borders to all immigrants. Lehman asserts that open borders would benefit America's economy by increasing competition, which would result in the lowering of both unskilled workers' wages and the cost of goods. The author contends that allowing unlimited immigration would lead to increased consumer purchasing power, enhanced living standards, and a more competitive labor market. Lehman is an adjunct professor of economics and Western civilization at Indiana Wesleyan University in Marion.

As you read, consider the following questions:

1. Why would domestic laborers not be harmed by lower wages, in Lehman's opinion?
2. What is Lehman's reply to the argument that immigrants would cross open borders and overload the welfare system?
3. According to the author, why is it dangerous to expand government powers for the sake of preserving tradition?

Thomas E. Lehman, "Coming to America: The Benefits of Open Immigration," *Freeman*, December 1994. (Endnotes of the original article have been omitted here.) Reprinted by permission of the *Freeman*.

For centuries, the American culture has been a beacon of hope to the oppressed peoples of collectivist economies and authoritarian or totalitarian governments throughout the world. Why then do the American people—descendants of immigrants, beneficiaries of open and unregulated immigration, whose culture, economy, government, and way of life are so deeply tied to open borders—exude such a passion against free immigration? Why do they wish so desperately to deny late twentieth-century immigrants the benefits to which their own eighteenth- and nineteenth-century ancestors were privileged? What do Americans have against open borders?

American immigration policy is a labyrinth of regulations and barriers to free travel and migration. One wishing to enter this country must possess all the legal and "proper" documentation in order to be permitted entry. The poverty-stricken and homeless foreigners who expect to benefit most from immigrating into the American economy rarely possess resources adequate for legal entry. Hence, they are denied. Such immigration policy is based upon a xenophobic confusion regarding economics, the mobility of labor, the American welfare state, and cultural diversity.

Immigration and Labor

Many Americans argue that free immigration would destroy "working class" Americans' ability to earn a living. They claim that allowing free and open borders to any and all immigrants would put decent, hard-working Americans out of work. Perhaps what these Americans really fear, however, is that someone will emerge from the "immigrant class" who would be willing to work for less than they while producing equal or greater output.

The present immigration policy of the United States amounts to nothing less than a tariff or barrier to entry on the commodity of labor, and harms American consumers in the same manner as tariffs and trade barriers on other capital or consumer goods.

A policy of open immigration would indeed force unskilled American laborers to compete for their jobs at lower wages. However, far from being an evil, this is a desirable outcome, one which should form the basis for a new immigration policy. By inviting competition into the American labor markets, artificially inflated labor costs could be eliminated and a greater level of labor efficiency could be achieved.

As the cost of labor (itself a cost of production) decreased, entrepreneurs and producers could produce more efficiently, enabling them to offer products and services at lower prices as they compete for consumers' dollars. Lower prices in turn increase the purchasing power of the American consumer, and thus enhance living standards for everyone. This is happening even now as some small business owners use "illegal" immi-

121

grant labor to lower their operating costs and thus lower consumer prices, as writer John S. DeMott explained in *Nation's Business* in December 1994: "Small-business executives do agree that some of their competitors who knowingly or unknowingly hire illegal immigrants use the cheap labor to undercut prices of business owners who play by the rules."

The Right to Immigrate

The right of persons to enjoy and share in the benefits of the earth is an integral part of [Catholic social] teaching. The right to move across borders to escape political persecution or in search of economic survival is explicitly part of that tradition.

Catholic social teaching takes what many view to be a counter-cultural position on this matter and insists that the right to immigrate is more fundamental than that of nations to control their borders.

Roger Mahony, *America*, November 27, 1993.

This is good for both consumers and the economy at large. As immigration makes the American labor market more competitive, costs of production are reduced and prices decline. In the long run, even the domestic laborer who is forced to lower his wage demands is not any worse off, since what he loses in terms of lower nominal wages he may well regain in terms of lower prices on the goods and services he purchases as a consumer. Meanwhile, everyone else benefits, and no one is privileged at the coerced expense of anyone else.

Immigration and Welfare

Another argument used in favor of immigration controls concerns the American welfare system and its potential abuse by immigrants who migrate into America merely to feed at the public trough of social services. The claim is made that the welfare system, not potential economic freedom, is the lure which draws immigrants into the American economy. Immigrants—unproductive, slothful, and indigent—constitute a dead-weight loss on the American economy, and further increase the tax burden on productive Americans. Therefore, we must police our borders and keep out the undesirables.

This argument is statistically and theoretically flawed. Contrary to prevailing public opinion, current immigrants do not "abuse" the public welfare system, even in the areas where immigration (legal or illegal) is most concentrated. In fact, immigrants have little effect on the current system of taxation and wealth redistribution. As Julian Simon relates:

> Study after study shows that small proportions of illegals use government services: free medical, 5 percent; unemployment insurance, 4; food stamps, 1; welfare payments, 1; child schooling, 4. Illegals are afraid of being caught if they apply for welfare. Practically none receive social security, the costliest service of all, but 77 percent pay social security taxes, and 73 percent have federal taxes withheld. . . . During the first five years in the United States, the average immigrant family receives $1404 (in 1975 dollars) in welfare compared to $2279 received by a native family.

Some may disagree with these statistics. Others would no doubt argue that if immigration controls were eliminated and borders completely unpoliced, a massive number of immigrants would enter the United States and overload the welfare system, causing taxes and the national debt to skyrocket. Certainly this is a possibility. But, even if we grant this argument the benefit of the doubt and concede that unrestricted immigrants would indeed flood the welfare system, the answer to the problem lies not in closing off the borders or "beefing up" border security. The answer lies in eliminating the American welfare state, and prohibiting anyone, native or immigrant, from living at the coerced expense of another.

Immigration and Culture

A final argument against immigration comes surprisingly from those generally supportive of liberty and the philosophy of the limited state. These critics are concerned for the preservation of what they see as a distinct American culture and its traditional heritage of European-style limited government and market economies. Their fear is that this traditional culture is being sabotaged by an influx of immigrants who are unfamiliar with and perhaps even hostile toward its institutional framework. They contend that immigrants of the late-twentieth-century variety do not possess the same ethnic characteristics of earlier immigrants, and therefore do not have an appreciation for the "American way of life." Such an argument suggests that recent immigrants who hail from Third World nations controlled by regimes of despotism have no understanding of the traditional institutions that have made America great. Allowing these immigrants of vastly different culture and ethnic heritage into the United States will result in a grave polarization of our society into racial enclaves that will run roughshod over our most sacred political and economic institutions.

To political conservatives, and even some libertarians, this argument may appear compelling at first blush. However, it is flawed. First, preserving "tradition" merely for the sake of tradition is pointless. The idea of tradition is meaningless unless we define the essence of that tradition in terms of the ideas that comprise it. Tradition alone is not what has made America great. Rather, it has been the reciprocal relationship between a limited state and economic and social liberty that has made the American way of life so coveted—in other words, the philosophy of liberty underlying the American tradition.

Expanding the power of government in order to preserve tradition is a sure path to the destruction of liberty. Americans ought to be particularly aware of this fact since the American tradition is bound together so tightly with the philosophy of freedom and limited government.

Yet, it is not the first time Americans have been down this road. U.S. public education began as a concerted effort to preserve the Protestant "traditions" of the American culture against the perceived threat of Catholicism. By subjecting the education establishment to the decisions of legislators and bureaucrats in local, state, and eventually national governments, Protestants hoped to stem the tide of Catholicism flowing into America on a nineteenth-century wave of immigration. As Samuel L. Blumenfeld relates:

> There was another reason why the Protestant religionists decided to join the secularists [socialists] in promoting the public school movement. They shared a common concern with, if not fear of, the massive Catholic immigration to the United States during that period. . . . [It was] argued that Protestants had to put aside sectarian differences and unite to defend Protestant republican America against the "Romish designs."

By making schools public rather than private, Protestants sought to use the power of the state to exclude the teachings and influence of Catholicism on their children, thereby preserving the Protestant "tradition" in America by way of majority vote. In retrospect, the bankruptcy of the American public education system ought to serve as a somber reminder that expanding state power to preserve "tradition" is a sure path to statism.

Based on Ideas

There is another flaw lurking in the argument that open immigration leads to the decline of a nation's cultural and institutional framework. Contrary to the anti-immigration position, the American traditions of limited government and free market economies are not based upon ethnic or racial origins. They are based upon ideas. Western cultures cannot suppose themselves to have a monopoly on the philosophy of liberty, nor can Americans argue that the political values of the limited state cannot be inculcated in non-American immigrants. The ideas of freedom that have created the American tradition can apply to any ethnic or racial make-up.

But what happens if, over time, America absorbs so many immigrants that, through their influence, the ideas of limited government and the free market economy become diluted? What happens when our political system falls victim to immigrant forces that seek to expand government power? These are good questions. The fact remains, however, that these fears are now being realized, and the foes of liberty in America are largely home-grown. Twentieth-century Americans have turned their backs on the philosophy of the limited state. They have generally refused to acknowledge the advantages of a laissez-faire market economy. It is not the foreign element, but rather the domestic element that we should fear. Before we begin to castigate potential immigrants for the damage they may do to our freedoms, we need to acknowledge the damage we have already done on our own.

The answer is to return once again to a government "of laws and not of men." In other words, the state must be radically limited in power and scope, with only minimal duties which are explicitly defined. This will put state power beyond the reach of those individuals or voting blocs that would seek to exploit it for personal gain. We then would have no reason to fear immigrants, regardless of their ideological or political persuasion. Their ability to "sabotage" our freedoms would be removed not because we expand state power to keep them out, but because we diminish state power in all areas and allow them in.

Immigration and Freedom

Immigration policy should not be viewed differently than trade policy: free, unregulated, unpoliced, open borders, devoid of taxes, tariffs, or any other barrier to entry. This is the policy of freedom to which America owes her heritage. Unilateral free trade, free immigration, and free emigration, where individuals possess unobstructed and unregulated mobility and trade, is a cornerstone of a free society. In fact, the free movement of peoples is no less important than the freedoms of speech, expression, and association. Liberty is indivisible; the laws of economics apply equally to all peoples.

Americans must begin to accept the fact that free trade and open borders are to their utmost benefit. By embracing the philosophy of free immigration and free labor mobility, we benefit from the productivity, ingenuity, and entrepreneurship not only of those within our borders, but also of those from without. Expanding the division of labor into the international marketplace makes available a vastly enlarged array of resources, thus enhancing the living standards of everyone.

"One of the cornerstones of our fight against illegal immigration has been a get-tough policy at our borders."

America Is Committed to Controlling Illegal Immigration

Bill Clinton

In the following viewpoint, U.S. president Bill Clinton argues that his administration is committed to providing the resources necessary to reduce illegal immigration. Clinton contends that he has instructed executive officials to expand and strengthen a program to combat illegal immigration. Clinton maintains that this program, for which he has requested more than $1 billion from Congress, will better protect U.S. borders and identify and remove illegal immigrants.

As you read, consider the following questions:

1. What are the names of the three operations initiated to strengthen the U.S.-Mexico border, according to Clinton?
2. According to the author, when did sanctions against employers of illegal immigrants become law?
3. How much money did Clinton request from Congress to reimburse states for their share of illegal immigration-related costs?

Bill Clinton, "U.S. Efforts to Expand and Strengthen the Fight Against Illegal Immigration," *U.S. Department of State Dispatch*, February 13, 1995.

When I took office in 1993, I was determined to do a better job of dealing with the problem of illegal immigration. When I discussed with Janet Reno the possibility of her becoming attorney general, we had a talk about this, and we have been hard at work trying to fix a system that everyone agrees has serious problems.

The Vice President and I have been briefed by Attorney General Reno; Doris Meissner, the Commissioner of Immigration and Naturalization Service [INS]; our Secretary of Labor, Bob Reich; Maria Echaveste, the Director of the Wage and Hour Division of the Labor Department; Silvestre Reyes, Chief Border Patrol Agent of the El Paso Sector; Gus de la Vina, the Director of the Western Region of the Immigration and Naturalization Service; Doug Crum, the U.S. Border Chief; and George Weise, our Customs Commissioner.

After our meeting, I signed a presidential directive to the heads of all executive departments instructing them to very quickly expand and strengthen our program to reduce illegal immigration in four key areas: first, protecting our borders; second, protecting the interests of our workers in the workplace; third, removing more criminal aliens; and fourth, providing more assistance to the states which are burdened with the problem of illegal immigration.

Effective Approaches

For example, I have asked the attorney general to increase those elements of our border patrol strategy that are proving most effective, including the use of helicopters, night scopes, and all-terrain vehicles. I have asked the members of the Cabinet to create—for the first time—a national detention and removal plan to dramatically increase the identification and removal of deportable illegal aliens. These are just a few examples.

One of the cornerstones of our fight against illegal immigration has been a get-tough policy at our borders. We initiated Operation Hold the Line at El Paso, Operation Gatekeeper in San Diego, and Operation Safeguard in Arizona, all with one clear intention: to secure the Southwest border.

As we speak, these initiatives are making a substantial difference. Illegal immigration is down; crime is down, and my immigration budget and strategy build on that success. Here are the elements of the initiative:

First, I asked Congress for an additional $1 billion to fight illegal immigration in the 1996 fiscal year.

I want to emphasize that while most of the talk in February 1995 was about cutting the budget—and we do have $140 billion in budget cuts—there are some things we should spend more money on.

We recommended spending more money on education, on medical research in AIDS, on crime, in the community policing bill, and on veterans interests; and we recommended a billion more dollars to fight illegal immigration. Under the budgets already passed, we have added 1,000 new border patrol agents just in the Southwest. By the end of 1996, our Administration will have increased overall border personnel by 51% since 1993.

A Crackdown on Employers

Second, I have asked for more funds to protect American jobs by increasing the number of workplace investigators by 85%. Our Administration will begin to test different methods of helping employers verify a worker's employment authorization. This was one of the key recommendations of the Jordan Commission [U.S. Commission on Immigration Reform]. [The late] Barbara Jordan . . . sent us a letter endorsing the proposals in this package.

Unprecedented Action

The Clinton Administration has taken unprecedented action to toughen enforcement of our immigration laws and is eager to see enactment of legislation that furthers our efforts to control illegal immigration. . . .

Congress has responded to the Administration's call for resources to support our new initiatives and ongoing activities through the appropriations process. The Administration urged the Congress to enact immigration legislation in 1995 to provide the INS with additional tools and resources to build a seamless web of enforcement from the border to the workplace.

Doris Meissner, U.S. Newswire report, October 25, 1995.

The fact is that employer sanctions have been in the law on illegal immigration since 1986, but no prior administration made a serious attempt to enforce them. With this budget and with legislation sent to Congress, we will be able to crack down on employers who knowingly hire illegal immigrants. If we turn off the employment stream for illegal workers, far, far fewer of them will risk the difficult journey here.

Incidentally, our financial support package for Mexico over the long run also will reduce pressure on illegal immigration. With a healthier economy, the Mexican people will find more opportunities for jobs at home.

Third, I have asked for new funds to [triple] the deportation of criminal aliens. And, finally, ours is the first administration to reimburse states for a share of the costs that they bear related to illegal immigration, including the incarceration of illegal aliens. I have asked Congress for a total of $550 million for state reimbursement, which more than doubles the fund [as of February 1995].

Quick and Effective Action

Whether through the budget, the directive I have signed, or the legislation sent to Congress, our goals are the same: tougher border enforcement, more protection for American workers, faster deportation of criminal aliens, and additional assistance to the states. That is a comprehensive strategy that is already beginning to work and that will work much better if this plan is implemented by the Administration and by Congress. We need help from Congress to implement this plan.

I want Congress to move quickly on this issue, just as we have moved quickly on a number of fronts. I am proud of the speed the INS showed in February 1995 in moving 62 border patrol agents in 24 hours to Nogales, Arizona, to reinforce that border. In the future, if our budget becomes law, that kind of movement will not be necessary. For the first time ever, there will be a rapid-response team to enable the border patrol to react quickly to buildups at any particular border spot.

We have accomplished a lot since 1993. As I said in the 1995 State of the Union address, we are a nation of immigrants, and we should all be proud of it, but we are also a nation of laws. It is wrong and ultimately self-defeating for a nation of immigrants to permit the kind of abuse of our immigration laws that we have seen in recent years. There is too much of it, and we must do much more to stop it.

"It is hard to imagine any other country tolerating the kind of wholesale disregard of its laws that is commonplace along our border."

America Is Not Committed to Controlling Illegal Immigration

Gary P. Freeman

The federal government has been consistently unwilling to control America's borders and to reduce the number of illegal immigrants, Gary P. Freeman argues in the following viewpoint. Freeman contends that special-interest groups that favor expanded immigration, such as business interests and ethnic and civil rights groups, have influenced the U.S. government to make a weak commitment to controlling illegal immigration. Freeman is an associate professor of government at the University of Texas in Austin and the author of two books on immigration.

As you read, consider the following questions:

1. What is the main belief of Pessimistic Realists, in Freeman's opinion?
2. In the author's opinion, what are the effects of disregarding immigration laws?
3. According to Freeman, what is the purpose of employer sanctions?

Excerpted from Gary P. Freeman, "The Fiction of Uncontrollable Borders," *Spectrum*, Winter 1994. Copyright 1994 by The Council of State Governments, Lexington, Ky. Reprinted with permission from *Spectrum: The Journal of State Government*.

In 1993 a government agency that had for years routinely failed to achieve its objectives suddenly began to succeed. A newly appointed director of the El Paso sector of the Border Patrol decided to bring to a halt the daily crossings that had made the area an entry point for thousands of illegal migrants. No remarkable new techniques were employed. Instead, existing procedures were used more effectively. Simply by paying overtime to have agents guard the Rio Grande around the clock, the number of people trying to enter the country illegally fell to a trickle.

The turnaround was so abrupt that some critics of the initiative seemed unwilling to accept the evidence. A lawyer involved in migrant affairs insisted almost wistfully [in the *Austin American Statesman*] that "[t]he bottom line is there is no way to stop immigration from Mexico short of shooting people or building a Berlin Wall."

Even if Operation Hold the Line is no more than a temporary blip in the longer curve of illegal migration to the United States, it is an instructive episode. It raises the possibility that we can, contrary to the dominant political rhetoric of the day, control illegal immigration.

Pessimistic Realism

Political discussion about illegal immigration is dominated by what might be called "Pessimistic Realism," though as we shall see there is more pessimism than realism to these ideas. Pessimistic Realists hold that short of extreme measures that would not be feasible politically or constitutionally the United States is powerless to prevent massive violation of her borders.

Pessimistic Realism is based on assumptions about the nature of the immigration pressures we face and viable strategies for dealing with them. With respect to the first, it holds that we must accept porous borders the same way some people learned to love the [nuclear] bomb during the Cold War. It is, however unpleasant, a fact of modern life. "Push" factors like population growth, poverty and the irrepressible desire of individuals for economic advancement create such ample supplies of potential migrants from the poor countries that they will defeat all attempts to keep them out. Furthermore, the structure of labor markets in the rich countries creates low-wage, low-skill jobs that natives avoid and that "pull" migrants to them.

Against these powerful currents, it is argued, law-enforcement measures are doomed to failure. Indeed, supposedly sophisticated commentators regard calls to take control of the borders through stricter policing as laughably naive and simplistic, if not dangerously nativist. We can apprehend illegals by the thousands, they warn, but they will only come back. Unless we are willing, in the language of the lawyer quoted above, to militarize the border on a scale heretofore uncontemplated, we will only slow but not stop the flow.

We need instead, Pessimistic Realists argue, to address the problem at its source by eliminating the conditions that create incentives for people to migrate. This involves changing those aspects of our foreign policy that produce refugees, and by adopting a mix of investment, trade and aid to improve the living standards of the migrant-producing areas of the world, especially Mexico and the Caribbean Basin.

Missing Important Points

Pessimistic Realism contains some elements of the truth, but it is ultimately defeatist. It casually dismisses the most direct and obvious methods of implementing immigration laws and recommends expensive, complicated and long-range measures unlikely to work. Who would deny that if living standards around the world were more equal there would be less migration? But that is to say little more than that one wishes the world were different. The insistence that only an attack at the root causes of immigration can succeed is less a radical proposal than a comforting thought. It paralyzes policy and assures that the status quo will not be altered.

Pessimistic Realism obscures the fact that, difficult as it may be, illegal migration can and should be reduced. While there are good reasons to pursue long-range strategies to reduce migration, I argue that we can do a much better job of controlling illegal immigration through direct enforcement. Broad and unqualified claims that this is impossible are unwarranted and often designed to forestall serious discussion of ways to deal with our border-control problems. . . .

Whatever the difficulties, compelling reasons exist to control our borders better. Illegal immigrants violate a reasonable and fair law. Disregard of the law, by those who break it and those who fail to enforce it, breeds cynicism and erodes respect for public institutions.

Stipulating who can enter the country is an aspect of national sovereignty that is jealously guarded by countries around the world. It is hard to imagine any other country tolerating the kind of wholesale disregard of its laws that is commonplace along our border. Our willingness to accept this situation diminishes our standing internationally. . . .

Immigration Policy Failures

Assuming we could agree that obtaining mastery over illegal immigration would be a good thing, how would we go about it? The answer to that question depends on an understanding of the sources of our immigration policy failures. The struggle between U.S. authorities and the masses of individuals seeking to enter or stay in the country without permission is only part of the illegal immigration story.

The U.S. government's attempts to control illegal immigration are as much opposed by domestic interests as by the migrants themselves. There are significant political forces in the United States opposed to effective border control. These groups often carry the day in conflicts over policy because of the expansionary bias in the politics of immigration. This bias produces a tendency for the government to pass weak immigration laws and to make only half-hearted attempts to enforce them. . . .

SMITH, YOU LISTEN FoR SMUGGLERS' SHiP RADIO SiGNALS.....JoHNSON, YOU LISTEN FoR UNDERGROUND TUNNEL DiGGING..... AND I'LL LISTEN FoR A COHERENT IMMiGRATiON POLiCY OUT OF WASHINGTON!

Steve Sack. Reprinted by permission: Tribune Media Services.

Immigration policy is a prerogative of the national government, but it is not typically a major issue in national political campaigns. To understand immigration policy, we must look to the way public officials interact with organized groups between elections.

In the group politics of immigration, those who favor expansion enjoy substantial advantages. Immigration may be said to produce diffuse costs and concentrated benefits. The relatively small number of persons who benefit have strong incentives to organize around the issue. Those who bear the costs are much less able to do so. We may think of immigration control as a public good. Like most public goods it has no clearly organized constituency. A form of client group politics emerges in which policy is made within a relatively tightly knit subsystem composed of private actors who enjoy a virtual monopoly on information and access to policy-makers.

Few individuals or groups publicly ally themselves with the cause of illegal migration, but many more give it tacit support. Immigration politics tend to produce odd coalitions. Historically, business has been the most important interest behind immigration expansion and against measures to curtail illegal entries and undocumented work. Agricultural growers play the leading role, relying heavily on seasonal workers from Mexico, but labor-intensive industry and small businesses, such as restaurants and laundries, are also important.

Other significant players include ethnic groups and a plethora of advocacy organizations concerned with humanitarian and civil rights. Ethnic groups, especially those of recent immigrant origin, are strongly attached to the principle of family reunion and see attempts to rein in immigration as a potential threat to their interests. The Hispanic Caucus in the Congress and national Hispanic organizations, such as the Mexican American Legal Defense and Education Fund, are critical of policies designed to curtail illegal migration. Immigrant and refugee advocacy groups monitor the activities of the Immigration and Naturalization Service carefully and often use the courts to challenge official policies.

Ignoring the Public

Politicians heed the demands of these groups and ignore the general public because it is in their interest to do so. Expansionists reward them with contributions and votes, while organized restrictionists are too weak to punish them. Politicians believe it is inappropriate to make electoral hay out of appeals related to immigration restriction. To do so is to lay oneself open to charges of racism and xenophobia. In these days of heightened sensibility to ethnic concerns, few are willing to take the risk.

Since the Los Angeles riots in May 1992, California politicians, including the governor and both U.S. senators, have been outspoken about illegal migration. But what is really remarkable in a country taking in three-quarters of a million legal and probably that many more illegal immigrants every year is that these California politicians are in the minority.

The expansionary politics of immigration produces policies that are more liberal than the general public prefers, have inadequate enforcement provisions and are haphazardly implemented. The chief reason it is premature to conclude that illegal immigration cannot be significantly reduced is because it has never been seriously tried.

Ineffective Agencies and Laws

The Immigration and Naturalization Service and its Border Patrol are among the weakest agencies in the federal government. Spending on enforcement activities, especially the Border Patrol, went up markedly in the early 1980s and received another substantial boost with the passage of the Immigration Reform and Control Act of 1986. Nevertheless, it did not keep pace with the growth of the federal budget or of the agency's responsibilities.

The Clinton administration added more than 600 Border Patrol officers and took other steps to shore up the agency. The saga in El Paso suggests that ample resources efficiently deployed can make an immediate impact.

Nothing has done more to erode public confidence in the ability of the government to handle illegal migration than the failure of the Immigration Reform and Control Act to make substantial inroads on the problem. The act was a mixed bag that resulted in amnesty for more than 3 million persons, with provisions for the further entry of their families. But it had only a brief and limited effect on illegal movement across the southern border.

The centerpiece of the control aspect of the law was employer sanctions, civil penalties imposed on employers who knowingly hire undocumented workers. Sanctions are a common device in other industrial democracies, where they have met some success. If they are to be effective, however, there must be a reliable and easy method of determining eligibility to work. Efforts to provide for a counterfeit-proof identity card in the legislation failed because of opposition from minority groups and civil libertarians. Without such a card, employers apparently relied on more informal techniques, such as the physical appearance of job candidates, which was prohibited by the law.

Now a coalition of employers and ethnic groups is seeking, for often contradictory reasons, to repeal sanctions. Their complaint that sanctions have not worked rings hollow in light of their role in emasculating the program. A zero-tolerance policy toward illegal immigration makes no sense. We can live with a certain level of movement. But there is no reason to throw up our hands, as the Pessimistic Realists counsel, and concede control over our borders to unelected noncitizens.

We need to raise immigration to the status of high politics where it can be fully and openly debated in national campaigns. That is surely where it belongs. For with an estimated 80 million people on the move around the globe, the United States will remain the focus of the aspirations of a large portion of the peoples of the world.

"We believe the national border control strategy shows promise for reducing illegal entry."

America Should Continue to Strengthen the U.S.-Mexico Border

Laurie E. Ekstrand

Beginning in 1993, the U.S. Border Patrol reinforced its El Paso and San Diego sectors with additional agents and border fences. In the following viewpoint, Laurie E. Ekstrand argues that this strategy has reduced illegal immigration through these ports of entry and promises to be effective along the rest of America's southwest border. Ekstrand is the associate director of the Administration of Justice Issues in the General Government Division of the General Accounting Office. The following viewpoint is excerpted from testimony Ekstrand presented to a March 1995 congressional hearing on border security.

As you read, consider the following questions:

1. What narcotics are being smuggled across the southwest border, according to Ekstrand?
2. In the author's opinion, what focus have the El Paso and San Diego border initiatives taken?
3. According to Ekstrand, what are the four phases of the INS border control strategy?

From House Subcommittee on Immigration and Claims, of the Committee on the Judiciary, *Border Security*, 104th Cong., 1st sess., March 10, 1995, Serial No. 13.

I am pleased to discuss our December 1994 report on the United States' efforts to secure the southwest border. Specifically, our report discusses (1) the extent of the threat from drug smuggling and illegal immigration and (2) ways to enhance security between the ports of entry. My testimony includes some follow-up data we collected from the Immigration and Naturalization Service (INS) since we concluded our review in September 1994.

Although the full extent of drug smuggling and illegal immigration is unknown, both pose a serious threat along the southwest border. Experts estimate that most of the cocaine and most of the illegal aliens entering the United States enter from Mexico across the southwest border. Despite law enforcement efforts, the flow of drugs continues, and, unless border control efforts become more effective, illegal immigration is expected to increase through the year 2005.

To enhance security along the southwest border, a 1993 Sandia National Laboratories study, commissioned by the Office of National Drug Control Policy (ONDCP), recommended that the Border Patrol focus on preventing illegal entry instead of apprehending aliens once they have entered the country. This study recommended prevention measures, such as multiple barriers, enhanced check point operations, and enhanced electronic surveillance equipment, which would significantly increase the difficulty of crossing the border illegally. A January 1989 study made similar recommendations.

In August 1994, the INS Commissioner approved a national Border Patrol strategic plan that focuses on preventing illegal entry. INS' national strategy builds on the successes that its San Diego and El Paso sectors have reportedly had in reducing illegal entry. INS plans to implement its strategy in phases over several years, concentrating initially in the two areas that traditionally had the greatest illegal activity—San Diego and El Paso. The strategy contains various indicators with which INS plans to measure the success of its efforts.

The Border Patrol's Mission

Within INS, the Border Patrol is the agency responsible for securing the border between the ports of entry. The Border Patrol's mission is to maintain control of the international boundaries between the ports of entry by detecting and preventing smuggling and illegal entry of aliens into the United States. In addition, in 1991, ONDCP designated the Border Patrol the primary agency for narcotics interdiction between the ports of entry.

To accomplish its mission, the Border Patrol (1) patrols the international boundaries and (2) inspects passengers and vehicles at checkpoints located along highways leading from border areas, at bus and rail stations, and at air terminals. The Border Patrol uses vehicles and aircraft to patrol areas between the ports of entry and electronic equipment, such as sensors and low-light-level televisions, to detect illegal entry into the country. The Border Patrol carries out its mission in 21 sectors. Nine of these sectors are located along the southwest border with Mexico. As of September 30, 1994, about 3,747 agents were assigned to these 9 sectors, representing 88 percent of Border Patrol agents nationwide.

Drug Smuggling

Although the full extent is unknown, drug smuggling is a serious threat along the southwest border. The Department of State's 1993 *International Narcotics Control Strategy Report* indicated that Mexico is a transit country for South American cocaine destined for the United States and a major country of origin for heroin and marijuana. According to the report, between 50 and 70 percent of the cocaine smuggled into the United States transited Mexico, entering primarily by land across the southwest border. In addition, about 23 percent of the heroin smuggled into the United States originated in Mexico.

INS data showed that Border Patrol narcotics seizures along the southwest border have risen. Between fiscal years 1990 and 1993, the number of Border Patrol narcotics seizures rose from around 4,200 to approximately 6,400, an increase of about 50 percent. The amount of cocaine seized nearly doubled from about 14,000 pounds in 1990 to about 27,000 pounds in 1993.

According to a June 1992 Operation Alliance report, the primary smuggling route across the southwest border was by land. The report pointed out that although cocaine was the primary drug threat, followed by marijuana, the heroin threat was growing. The report stated that in spite of law enforcement agencies' efforts to counter drug smuggling, the flow of drugs between the ports of entry along the southwest border continued due to vast open areas and a relatively low law enforcement presence. The report concluded that "our successes are insignificant when compared to the threat."

Illegal Immigration

Illegal immigration is also a serious threat to the United States. In 1993, we estimated that the total inflow of illegal aliens into this country in 1988 ranged from 1.3 million to 3.9 million. The major component of the inflow, 1.2 million to 3.2 million, was Mexicans crossing the southwest border, with most entering between the ports of entry. Much of the inflow represented short-term visits to the United States.

In June 1994, INS estimated there were about 3.8 million undocumented migrants residing in the United States. About half of these unlawful residents entered without documentation across the borders, while the other half entered lawfully as visitors but did not leave.

In fiscal year 1993, the San Diego and El Paso Border Patrol sectors accounted for two-thirds of the 1.2 million southwest border apprehensions. Our analysis of INS data showed that in fiscal year 1992, over half of all southwest border apprehensions occurred along only 18 of the 1,600 border miles—13 miles along the border between San Diego and Tijuana, Mexico, and 5 miles along the border between El Paso and Ciudad Juarez, Mexico. However, border control initiatives in San Diego and El Paso appear to have resulted in rerouting some illegal immigrants to other southwest border areas. For example, San Diego and El Paso's share of total southwest border apprehensions dropped from two-thirds in fiscal year 1993 to about one-half in fiscal year 1994.

Unless border control efforts become more effective, illegal immigration is expected to increase. In September 1993, we reported that the flow of illegal aliens across the southwest border is expected to increase because Mexico's economy is unlikely to absorb all of the new job seekers that are expected to enter the labor force. In testimony before the House Committee on Banking and Financial Services, both the Treasury Secretary and the Secretary of State expressed concern that the peso devaluation could increase illegal migration.

Prevention Strategy Has Widespread Support

The Border Patrol officials with whom we spoke (including the chief, acting deputy chief, San Diego and El Paso chief patrol agents, and a regional Border Patrol official) all agreed with the Sandia study's conclusion that the Border Patrol should focus on preventing illegal entry rather than on apprehending illegal aliens. In addition, officials of the El Paso Intelligence Center (EPIC), Operation Alliance, Joint Task Force Six (JTF-6), and the mayor and police officials of El Paso support the concept of trying to prevent entry rather than apprehending aliens.

This strategy is also in line with our past positions on controlling illegal immigration. In June 1993, we testified before this Committee that "the key to controlling the illegal entry of aliens is to prevent their initial arrival."

Both the San Diego and El Paso sectors have begun major border control initiatives that focus on preventing illegal entry rather than on apprehending aliens. Preliminary results in these two sectors suggest that the prevention strategy has reduced illegal entry in these sectors. Other benefits include less border crime, less confrontation between Border Patrol agents and illegal aliens, and strong public and government support.

In 1990, the San Diego sector's chief patrol agent began an initiative to erect physical barriers, primarily to deter drug smuggling. With the assistance of JTF-6, the San Diego sector installed 10-foot welded steel fencing along approximately 13 miles of border where sector officials believed the majority of drugs and illegal aliens crossed within the sector. The new fence, completed in late 1993, is substantially stronger than previous chain link fencing. JTF-6 is also installing high-intensity lights and a second and third fence at strategic locations along the same 13 miles. As of February 7, 1995, JTF-6 had installed lights along about 4½ of the 13 miles.

Although the San Diego sector's border control initiative has not been fully implemented, indications are that the tactics are reducing the number of aliens crossing the border illegally in the San Diego area. Sector apprehensions were down 20 percent in fiscal year 1994 compare to 1992 and dropped below 1990 levels, the year the sector began implementing its border control tactics. Apprehensions decreased even though the sector increased the amount of time spent on border enforcement nearly 41 percent between 1990 and 1994.

The Border Strategy Works

The benefits of a secure border are clear and irrefutable. Following initial protests to the El Paso [fortified border] operation, border crime and automobile thefts in the metropolitan area dropped markedly. The relationship between Border Patrol agents and the community improved as agents focused on securing the border area rather than patrolling the city looking for aliens and smugglers. Even in San Diego, following initial protests against the reinforced fencing, assaults on Border Patrol agents plummeted and the number of border murders dropped to zero in one year. The strategy stopped drive-through traffic, forcing drug and alien smugglers east to other, less fortified sectors. With the forward deployment of the Border Patrol, we could all but halt illegal foot traffic in San Diego—and in other sectors as well.

Duncan Hunter, statement to the House of Representatives Subcommittee on Immigration and Claims, March 10,1995.

Also, apprehensions at highway checkpoints away from the border declined 24 percent between fiscal years 1990 and 1993 even though the amount of time spent performing traffic checks increased 22 percent.

During our review, we toured the most heavily trafficked portion of the San Diego sector border and found visible evidence of the tactics' effect on illegal border crossing. Before the border control tactics, hundreds of aliens would line up along the U.S. side of the border during daylight hours, waiting for an opportunity to go northward. However, after the border patrol tactics were initiated, large groups of aliens no longer waited during the day to cross at night, which according to a Border Patrol official is now typical. Also, formerly there were large gaps in border fencing allowing aliens to easily cross the border. However, these gaps in the fencing have now been closed.

El Paso's Operation Hold-the-Line

Before September 1993, like San Diego, the El Paso sector's strategy emphasized apprehending aliens rather than preventing illegal entry. However, as apprehensions increased so did the opportunities for confrontation between illegal aliens and El Paso Border Patrol agents. These increased opportunities for confrontation led to allegations of abuse against agents.

Under the sector's apprehension strategy, El Paso's chief patrol agent told us that the border area was in "complete chaos." The chief estimated there were up to 8,000 to 10,000 illegal border crossings daily, and only 1 out of 8 aliens was apprehended. In addition, El Paso police officials estimated illegal aliens had a significant impact on the city's crime rates, committing 75 to 80 percent of all auto thefts, as well as many burglaries.

El Paso's chief patrol agent began an initiative in September 1993 to change the sector's border control strategy to one of preventing illegal entry. The sector stationed all available agents immediately at a 20-mile stretch of the border in highly visible Border Patrol vehicles. The primary goal of the new strategy—Operation Hold-the-Line—was preventing significant numbers of aliens from entering the El Paso metropolitan area. Those who still tried to cross the border illegally were routed to less populated areas where they could be more easily apprehended.

El Paso sector officials cited several indications that its new prevention strategy is working. For example, according to the Border Patrol, the number of aliens attempting to illegally cross the border through the El Paso sector has decreased significantly. According to the chief patrol agent, before Operation Hold-the-Line, there were up to 10,000 illegal border crossings daily. In February 1994, the sector estimated that only about 500 people a day were illegally crossing the border. A March 1994 sector intelligence report indicated the strategy had deterred many aliens in Mexico's interior from coming to the El Paso border area.

There has been a sharp drop in El Paso sector apprehensions since implementation of its strategy. The El Paso sector's illegal alien apprehensions in fiscal year 1994 were down 72 percent compared to fiscal year 1993. Two factors influencing this decrease are the deterrent effect of the prevention strategy and the rerouting of some illegal aliens to other southwest border areas.

The El Paso public strongly supports the sector's strategy. A poll taken in February 1994 showed 84 percent of those polled were in favor of the strategy. Also, police officials attribute a drop in certain crimes to Operation Hold-the-Line. For example, there were nearly one-third fewer burglaries and one-fourth fewer motor vehicle thefts in the 3 months after the operation began in September 1993 than in the same 3 months in 1992.

Two studies also concluded that Operation Hold-the-Line has been successful in deterring illegal immigration in El Paso. A December 1993 study of Operation Hold-the-Line by the Center for Immigration Studies concluded that the operation "has proven to be successful" and the preventative deployment was "both more humane and more effective." According to this study, the operation represented a viable long-term approach to more successful border control.

A July 1994 study requested by the Commission on Immigration Reform found that Operation Hold-the-Line significantly reduced illegal crossings, and resulted in less crime and fewer allegations against Border Patrol agents. In addition, the strategy appeared to have broad public support.

However, the operation may be having different effects depending on the type of illegal border crosser. For example, the operation has had less of a deterrent effect on those who illegally cross the border to find work in other locations in the United States. According to the study, these crossers have shifted their crossing points to other border locations. Conversely, illegal crossers who engage in street vending and low-level criminal activities have been substantially deterred from crossing the border. The operation has also had some unintended consequences. For example, in some cases, those crossers who normally would cross the border daily to work illegally in El Paso have extended their stay in El Paso to reduce the number of times that they illegally cross the border.

Increased Apprehensions

According to an El Paso Assistant Chief Patrol Agent, the sector has experienced an increase in apprehensions. For the first 4 months of fiscal year 1995, apprehensions were 29 percent higher than the same time the previous year (26,900 versus 20,900). The official attributed this rise to increased alien smuggling, aliens attempting to return to the U.S. after the holidays, and the devaluation of the Mexican peso. However, although the El Paso sector is [as of March 1995] averaging about 6,700 alien apprehensions per month, this is still significantly lower than the 24,000 per month the sector averaged in fiscal year

1993, before Operation Hold-the-Line.

The San Diego and El Paso sectors' initiatives appear to have resulted in rerouting drugs and illegal aliens to other parts of the southwest border.

Interviews with apprehended illegal aliens have revealed that smugglers are now telling those traveling from the interior of Mexico that it is easier to cross into Nogales, Arizona, rather than into San Diego or El Paso, according to Tucson's Deputy Chief Patrol Agent. In addition, according to the deputy, some smugglers are reported to be moving their operations from San Diego to Nogales.

A comparison of Tucson and El Paso sector apprehensions appears to support the premise that the San Diego and El Paso initiatives have increased illegal entry through other southwest border sectors. Since the start of the initiative in the El Paso sector, Tucson sector apprehensions have increased about 50 percent (about 93,000 in fiscal year 1993 compared to 139,000 in fiscal year 1994). El Paso apprehensions, on the other hand, have dropped 72 percent (from about 286,000 to about 80,000 over the same period).

A Shift in Illegal Crossings

Another indication that illegal alien entry may be moving to other sectors is that while the San Diego sector's fiscal year 1994 apprehensions were 15 percent lower than in fiscal year 1993, and El Paso's were down 72 percent over the same period, apprehensions in the remaining seven southwest border sectors increased about 14 percent.

Drug trafficking has also apparently been affected. According to EPIC's *December 1993 Monthly Threat Brief*, El Paso's Operation Hold-the-Line has led to changes in smuggling methods. Instead of fording the Rio Grande, some smugglers have attempted to move drugs through ports of entry and to areas east and west of El Paso, around the sector's 20-mile line of agents.

According to a San Diego sector official, the new fence has virtually eliminated drug and alien smugglers driving across the border in the San Diego sector. However, the sector has noticed an increase in drug smuggling in the mountainous areas east of San Diego. In addition, the amount of cocaine seized in the El Centro sector, the sector adjacent to San Diego, increased dramatically from 698 pounds in fiscal year 1991 to nearly 18,000 pounds in fiscal year 1993.

On February 5, 1995, President Bill Clinton directed INS to send 62 additional Border Patrol agents to Nogales to combat an unprecedented rise in illegal border crossings there. According to a White House statement, the administration attributes this dramatic increase to the California and Texas border control initiatives, as well as the devaluation of the Mexican peso. The additional agents are being reassigned from the Canadian border, as well as from interior Border Patrol stations.

INS' National Border Control Strategy

In August 1994, the INS Commissioner approved a national Border Patrol strategic plan for gaining control of the nation's borders. The strategy focuses on preventing illegal entry and builds on the success INS has reportedly had in San Diego and El Paso. INS plans to put more agents along the border and use more lighting, fencing, and other barriers. On the basis of the national border control strategy, each southwest border sector developed its own strategy identifying specific actions that need to be taken.

INS plans to use a phased approach to implementing its border control strategy. In its first phase, INS plans to focus its resources in the two sectors where most illegal immigration has traditionally occurred—San Diego and El Paso. As border control continues to improve in San Diego and El Paso, INS anticipates that other sectors will continue to experience an increase in illegal entry. Therefore, the second phase targets the Tucson sector and south Texas—areas that are expected to be most affected by the enhancements at San Diego and El Paso. The third phase targets the rest of the southwest border, and phase four targets the rest of the U.S. border. According to a Border Patrol official, INS is [as of March 1995] transitioning from phase one to phase two. . . .

INS officials told us that it will take several years to implement the strategy and that INS did not have a specific time frame or cost figures for these improvements. INS officials believe that technology improvements, such as improved fencing and surveillance cameras, would make border control strategies more effective. According to the Chief of the Border Patrol, these improvements would reduce the need for significant numbers of additional agents. . . .

We believe the national border control strategy shows promise for reducing illegal entry since the strategy (1) builds on the reported success the San Diego and El Paso sectors have had in reducing illegal immigration, (2) is consistent with recommendations made in previous comprehensive studies conducted by border control and physical security experts, and (3) has widespread public and government support. However, since it will take several years to implement the strategy, it is too early to tell what impact it will eventually have on drug smuggling and illegal immigration along the southwest border. Tightening border control in some sectors seems to put added stress on other sectors. This speaks to the need for a comprehensive approach along the entire border.

6

"Tighter border control . . . actually increases the incentive to successfully cross the border, and once across, to stay longer."

America's U.S.-Mexico Border Strategy Has Been Counterproductive

Peter Andreas

Many critics of illegal immigration advocate strict border enforcement as a means of reducing the number of immigrants who enter America illegally. In the following viewpoint, Peter Andreas argues that this approach has proven unsuccessful. Attempts to stop illegal immigrants in some areas have merely diverted them to other areas, he maintains. Moreover, he contends, many immigrants who are caught and deported simply try again. Andreas was a Ph.D. student in government at Cornell University in Ithaca, New York, when this article was originally published in 1994.

As you read, consider the following questions:

1. According to Andreas, what are the official estimates of the number of illegal immigrants in the United States?
2. In the author's opinion, what is the conflict between free trade and suppressing illegal immigration?
3. What is the primary responsibility of the National Guard along the border, according to Andreas?

From Peter Andreas, "The Making of Amerexico: (Mis)Handling Illegal Immigration," *World Policy Journal*, vol. 11, no. 2, Summer 1994. Reprinted by permission.

In the United States, the quintessential nation of immigrants, the influx of new arrivals has sparked a growing nativist backlash. While a Gallup poll in 1965 showed that only 33 percent of Americans believed too many immigrants were entering the country, the number increased to 42 percent in 1977, 49 percent in 1986, and 65 percent in the summer of 1993. In a *Newsweek* poll in late July 1993, 59 percent of respondents said immigration was good for America in the past, but 60 percent thought it was a bad thing today. While most immigrants arrive legally, national attention and frustration have focused on those who come without a formal invitation. No one really knows how many people are in the United States illegally, but official estimates put the number somewhere above 3 million, with hundreds of thousands more entering each year.

The tension between government restrictions and illegal entry is sharpest along the 1,945-mile border the United States shares with Mexico, the longest point of contact between a developed and a developing country in the world. Each year, the U.S. Border Patrol apprehends about one million people attempting to enter the United States from Mexico. Border apprehension rates have increased by a multiple of 15 over the last 30 years.

A Porous Border

As political pressure has mounted to "do something" about illegal immigration, lax border control has been targeted as the source of the problem. Sen. Alan Simpson (R-WY) has put it rather starkly: "The first duty of a sovereign nation is to control its borders. We do not. . . . Uncontrolled immigration is one of the greatest threats to the future of this country." This sentiment echoes the warning voiced by former CIA director William Colby in the late 1970s: "The most obvious threat [for the U.S.] is the fact that . . . there are going to be 120 million Mexicans by the end of the century. . . . [The Border Patrol] will not have enough bullets to stop them." The influx of illegal drugs across the border in recent years has only reinforced such "fortress America" sentiments and has been used to justify introducing the military and the National Guard along the border. The missions of drug control and immigration control have consequently become increasingly intertwined.

While government officials rush to barricade our border with Mexico, their fight to lower economic barriers along that same border stands in sharp contrast. In other words, even as officials have moved to close the border (to the illegal flow of people), they have moved to open it (to the legal flow of goods through the North American Free Trade Agreement). Ironically, while NAFTA promotes free trade between the United States and Mexico, it does not reduce tariffs on what is arguably Mexico's most important export: people. Far from being eliminated, such tariffs are being increased. This does not, however, necessarily make them more effective. Trying to discourage the mobility of people while at the same time encouraging the mobility of virtually everything else is a recipe for policy frustration. . . .

More Resources

The U.S.-Mexico border is notorious for its porousness, even though in recent years the United States has significantly beefed up border control. While funding for the Border Patrol grew slowly during much of the postwar period, its budget jumped 82 percent between 1986 and 1991—from $164 million to $299 million. In contrast, the 1980 budget was only $77 million (less than the budget of the Baltimore police department). In response to growing fears that the United States had "lost control" of its borders, IRCA [the 1986 Immigration Reform and Control Act] increased the number of Border Patrol agents in 1986 from 2,500 to about 4,800. In July 1993, President Bill Clinton proposed an additional 12 percent increase in the number of agents, and in February 1994, he proposed another 30 percent increase in the number of Border Patrol agents on the U.S.-Mexico frontier.

U.S. border-control strategists have long maintained that "prompt apprehension and return to country of origin is a positive deterrent to illegal entry and related violations" [as Sherrie Kossoudji wrote in *Demography* in May 1992]. There is, however, good reason to be skeptical of such claims. Most illegal immigrants simply try again—indeed, it is not uncommon for an illegal immigrant to be detained more than once in one day. As one young Mexican told the Border Patrol agent who caught and handcuffed him as he attempted to cross the border recently, "It doesn't matter how many times you catch me. I'll be back."

Contradictory Effects

Not only is the effectiveness of border control questionable, but there is growing evidence that intensified border enforcement has some contradictory effects. Many illegal immigrants make repeated trips between the United States and Mexico, often staying in the United States only long enough to earn a fixed amount of money. However, intensified border control has pressured immigrants to stay longer. The more difficult it is to cross the border, the more expensive the journey becomes. As border controls are tightened, illegal immigrants must rely increasingly on "coyotes"—professional smugglers—who take them across the border for a fee (the going rate to be transported to Los Angeles is about $700 per person). This fee must be paid whether or not the border crossing is successful. Thus, once detained by the Border Patrol and sent back to Mexico, illegal immigrants have even *more* of an incentive to try again, since the only way they can repay their debts to the smugglers is by earning the money in the United States.

The end result is that while tighter border control may reduce the number of trips made by illegal immigrants, it actually increases the incentive to successfully cross the border, and once across, to stay longer. Moreover, by forcing illegal immigrants to depend more on smugglers, border enforcement has unintentionally helped to create a highly profitable and increasingly sophisticated binational business in "human trafficking." Each tactic by the Border Patrol—such as deeper and longer ditches and stronger and higher fences—has been countered with new tactics by the smugglers.

No Barricades

Any initiative to build physical barriers between Mexico and the United States sets a frightening precedent. While a small wall may seem acceptable, more walls will inevitably follow. It frightens me to envision a 2000-mile wall dividing nations that are so culturally and economically interdependent. . . . [Walls] send the wrong signal from a nation that proclaims to be a free society.

If we want a long-term solution to the problems caused by large waves of poor immigrants, we need to focus upon the economic viability of poor countries. The borders of free and wealthy nations are never barricaded. Thus, we need to work toward helping Mexico to achieve the economic liberalization and the political openness that will ensure that Mexican citizens feel no need to look for a better life elsewhere. It is inhumane to prevent people from entering this nation if we do not use our considerable resources to create a better climate in their home nations.

Ronald D. Coleman, statement to the House of Representatives Subcommittee on Immigration and Claims, March 10, 1995.

Immigration officials nonetheless believe that the problem is not the border deterrence strategy itself but the inadequacy of resources devoted to making the strategy work. In the words of one Border Patrol official: "With a sufficient show of force you can stop it [illegal border crossings]. With enough manpower and technology, you can do it humanely and adequately." In congressional hearings, immigration officials endlessly discuss problems of bureaucratic coordination, personnel decisions, and equipment needs. The assumption is that more is better—that the obstacle is technical rather than inherent in the very nature of the border-control strategy. Yet while better training and equipment may indeed make the policy more *efficient*, they do not make it more *effective*.

The Balloon Effect

In an effort to prove the effectiveness of border enforcement, in September 1993 the Border Patrol in El Paso, Texas, initiated "Operation Blockade," in which more than 450 agents working overtime covered a 20-mile stretch of the border. As hoped, illegal border crossings in that area plummeted. One Border Patrol agent declared: "We've proven it works, that it's feasible, that it's practical, that it's enforceable, and that it's desirable. I think it will work anywhere that you're willing to commit and dedicate the resources." Yet suppressing the flow in one border area simply redirects it elsewhere; new crossing points for illegal immigrants have emerged on both sides of the 20-mile El Paso "blockade."

Meanwhile, a ten-foot-high steel border fence—which Mexicans have dubbed the "iron curtain"—is being completed along the border south of San Diego. "I think you could secure the border, the California-Mexico border, but the problem is going to pop up some other place, whether it's Texas, New Mexico, or some other place," notes Rep. Michael Kopetski (D-OR). "There's no end to it," concedes one Border Patrol agent. "We call it the balloon effect. You squeeze it here; it just goes over there." Indeed, the fence appears already to be causing problems for neighboring states. Arizona Border Patrol officials report that smugglers have begun to redirect illegal immigrants to cross at Nogales, Arizona. The Border Patrol blames the 30 percent rise in illegal crossings at the Arizona border in 1993 in part on greater enforcement in southern California. This has, predictably, prompted Arizona officials to consider building their own fences. But it will take a lot of fences to cover 2,000 miles.

Ultimately, however, efforts to "seal the border" are limited by the realities of high levels of transborder commerce—which will only increase under NAFTA. Officials are understandably torn between the conflicting goals of suppressing illegal flows and supporting legal flows. And as legal flows increase, it becomes more and more difficult to "weed out" the illegal flows. About 1,700 trucks cross the bridge over the Rio Grande from Juarez, Mexico, to El Paso, Texas, every day—the same site as the Border Patrol's "Operation Blockade." One Customs official in El Paso conceded that "most trucks that go through customs go through almost unimpeded." Under the trade agreement, trucking into the United States from Mexico will expand significantly, since Mexican truckers will eventually be able to travel anywhere in the United States and Canada. Trucks, of course, can carry illegal immigrants and drugs as easily as legal goods. U.S.

law enforcement officials believe that the biggest cocaine cache ever seized in the United States—a 21-ton supply found in a Los Angeles warehouse—belonged to the owner of one of Mexico's biggest trucking companies.

A Narrow Focus

Despite the serious limits and flaws of past and present U.S. policies, the current political climate favors policy escalation rather than re-evaluation. The inadequacy of border control has created its own self-perpetuating bureaucratic logic. As border deterrence fails to stem the tide of illegal entries, immigration officials understandably press for more resources. While border-control programs are carefully scrutinized in congressional hearings, these evaluations tend to be narrowly focused on operational concerns—equipment needs, numbers of arrests, and deployment of border agents. The viability of the overall mission remains largely unquestioned. Immigration officials, of course, have every incentive to promote rather than question their mission. From their narrow bureaucratic perspective, their only responsibility is to carry out their assigned task—even if their own individual "successes" (i.e., the number of illegal immigrants detained) fail to translate into a successful policy.

Answering calls to integrate the military into border control would only reinforce this "logic." One former army officer has suggested that, with the military looking for a new job in the post–Cold War era, "A more easily accomplished mission for existing forces would be patrolling the borders. It is, of course, absurd that the most powerful nation on earth cannot prevent a swarming land invasion by unarmed Mexican peasants. The U.S. Army is entirely capable of plugging the holes permanently, and border duty would be excellent military training." In 1981, the historical separation between law enforcement and the military on the border was terminated with several amendments to the Posse Comitatus Act. And in May 1986, the Justice Department concluded that the military could be used to help curb illegal immigration. The National Guard also operates along the border, primarily in an antidrug capacity, but there is growing political pressure for it to have a more direct role in immigration control.

"Do Not Enter"

Behind the bureaucratic logic of escalating border enforcement is a deeper political logic, revealed by the dynamics of the current immigration debate. Embedded in this policy debate are deeply held beliefs that both define the nature of the "immigrant problem" and limit the range of acceptable solutions. The guiding assumption is that the influx of illegal immigrants is a product of excessive U.S. generosity and lax border enforcement. Since illegal immigrants are presumed to be free-riding on American hospitality, the way to control illegal immigration is to pull up the welcome mat by putting a bigger "do not enter" sign along the border. "We can't afford to lose control of our own borders at a time when we are not adequately providing for the jobs, the health care, and the education of our own people," says President Clinton. California senator Dianne Feinstein has put it a bit more bluntly: "The day when America could be the welfare system for Mexico is gone. We simply can't afford it." She conveniently leaves unmentioned her state's reliance on Mexican labor.

Partisan politics play no small role in the escalation, compelling both Democrats and Republicans to take a hard line on illegal immigration. In an effort to ride—rather than be drowned by—the rising tide of alarm over illegal immigration, President Clinton held a news conference in July 1993 to announce new measures against illegal immigration, including 600 more Border Patrol agents. "We will make it tougher for illegal aliens to get into our country," Clinton promised. Yet Clinton was merely trying to stay ahead of Republican initiatives on Capitol Hill. An amendment by Representative Duncan Hunter (R-CA) to add 600 agents had passed through the House earlier in the month. In announcing the increases, Clinton noted, "It's certainly plain to anybody with eyes to see that the Border Patrol is drastically understaffed, breathtakingly understaffed." The president failed to mention that his budget had initially called for a cut of 93 Border Patrol agents. As soon as California governor Pete Wilson proposed cutting public services to illegal immigrants and denying citizenship to children born to illegals in the United States, his approval rating jumped ten points—the first rise in two years. Wilson vowed to make the illegal immigration problem a crusade. "I'm going to raise all the hell I can." Only a few years earlier, Wilson was pleading for a relaxation of border controls so that Mexican workers could cross the border to apply for special agricultural workers visas.

"A program to bring in temporary non-immigrant workers was tried—and succeeded—before."

America Should Admit Guest Farmworkers

Rael Jean Isaac

During World War II and until the early 1960s, the United States permitted hundreds of thousands of undocumented agricultural workers, mostly from Mexico, to work temporarily in America. In the following viewpoint, Rael Jean Isaac argues that this practice, called the "bracero" program, should be reinstituted to concurrently reduce illegal immigration and provide sufficient numbers of seasonal farmworkers. She contends that this program would benefit both growers of hand-picked seasonal crops and countries that are a source of illegal immigrants. Isaac writes about public policy for the *Wall Street Journal* daily newspaper.

As you read, consider the following questions:

1. How did an industry in fraudulent documents come about, in Isaac's opinion?
2. According to the author, why did the Kennedy administration end the bracero program?
3. Why do countries from which illegal immigrants come prefer a guest-worker program, according to Isaac?

Rael Jean Isaac, "Invite the Guest Workers Back," *Wall Street Journal*, November 5, 1995. Reprinted with permission of the *Wall Street Journal*; ©1995 Dow Jones & Company, Inc. All rights reserved.

The Republican leadership helped pass a new immigration bill early in 1996 to close loopholes in the Immigration Reform and Control Act (IRCA) of 1986 that have made it ineffective in curtailing illegal immigration. The House Agriculture Committee and the immigration subcommittee of the House Judiciary Committee scheduled joint hearings on how to make sure that the bill does not succeed *too* well, barring people needed to fill occupational gaps. The hearings focused especially on how to prevent immigration reform from devastating an important segment of U.S. agriculture—the fruit, vegetable and nursery growers who depend upon seasonal labor, an estimated 20% to 40% of it now illegal, to harvest their crops.

IRCA's strategy had been to legalize immigrants already here and then, by making employers who hired illegal aliens liable for stiff penalties, take away the jobs that lured others to follow. That strategy failed.

Fraudulent Documents

Congress, responding to critics who objected that applicants might be turned away simply because they appeared foreign, specified that employers were required to accept applicants with eligibility documents that "reasonably appear to be genuine." Indeed, they could face stiff penalties under anti-discrimination statutes if they did not. That produced an industry in fraudulent documents. In 1992 the IRCA-established Commission on Agricultural Workers reported that its researchers had visited flea markets in California where state identification cards, with photographs, sold for $10 and Social Security cards for $15.

In many parts of the country, employers have been happy to accept such documents. In agriculture, seasonal workers have been in critically short supply for decades. Even when national unemployment rates are high, welfare and unemployment benefits offer more attractive alternatives than physically demanding, short-term agricultural labor far from home. Yet despite progress in mechanization in crops like cotton, sugar cane, and tomatoes destined for processing, many of America's fruit and vegetables are still hand harvested. Growers need large numbers of workers for short periods at specific times: In the case of strawberries and salad tomatoes, there may be a window of only a few days in which to harvest the crop.

Now Congress plans to mandate the use of identity checks that would make document forgeries far more difficult. But how then are sufficient numbers of seasonal agricultural workers to be found?

The solution, a program to bring in temporary non-immigrant workers, was tried—and succeeded—before. There was a tremendous surge in the number of undocumented workers, chiefly

Mexican, from 1948 to 1954. The "immigration crisis" of that era was ended when the "bracero" program—which had been established, in cooperation with the Mexican government, during World War II to bring in replacement agricultural manpower as U.S. workers went to war and arms factories—was dramatically expanded. From 1955 to 1961 more than 300,000 Mexicans were admitted each year, reaching a peak of 445,000 in 1956 and remaining at more than 400,000 until 1959.

Successful Results

The results were immediate. In 1955 the number of illegals apprehended fell by 75% to just under 250,000 and the Immigration and Naturalization Service [INS] declared: "The so-called 'wetback' problem no longer exists. . . . The border has been secured." In 1956 the number of illegal entrants apprehended tumbled even more dramatically, dropping to 87,000. It was not until 1962, when the bracero program was being phased out, that the number of INS apprehensions again began to rise.

Matching Foreigners and Employers

Instead of spending money to hire more agents to hunt for illegal immigrants and detain them, Congress should set up a guest-worker program that matches foreigners with the employers who need them to fill the hard, low-paying jobs that Americans are loath to do. . . .

Foreign workers would sign up by occupation and be assigned to companies that needed them, with a maximum stay of perhaps three to five years. Although Congress would have to decide which countries would be involved, it is likely that most workers would come from Mexico, the Caribbean and Central America.

In approving guest-worker applicants, the Government might give priority to illegal aliens already working in the United States. Though some critics might complain that this rewards lawbreakers, it would be less of a boon for them than the permanent amnesty for illegals that was granted in the late 1980's.

Julian L. Simon, *New York Times*, June 1, 1995.

The role of the program in solving the border problem was well understood at the time. In October 1959, a group of consultants appointed by then-Secretary of Labor James Mitchell reported to Congress: "Almost one-half million Mexicans were brought into the country last year in an orderly, organized fashion to supplement the domestic farmworker force. The existence of such a legal system has facilitated the elimination of the illegal entry of Mexicans." Another important factor was grower cooperation with the INS, which was forthcoming because farmers could be assured of obtaining a legal work force.

The bracero program was ended by the Kennedy administration in response to pressures from organized labor and public interest groups, who argued that Mexicans took jobs away from domestic workers and depressed their wages. But within five years of the end of the bracero program, the number of domestic farm workers declined by an additional 400,000. Illegal immigrants once again filled the gap, and by 1980 INS apprehensions were once more close to the million mark.

The "H" Program

Today, the only surviving foreign worker program is the nearly defunct "H" program (named for the paragraph in which it is described in the immigration law) created by Congress in 1951. The program for agricultural workers—known as H2A—has primarily brought in workers from the Caribbean (chiefly Jamaicans) who have harvested, for example, sugar cane in Florida and apples on the East Coast. While the program was never large, in recent years the numbers have fallen sharply, from 30,000 in 1989 to about 11,000 in 1995. The reason is not hard to find. The Labor Department, which administers the program, is openly hostile to it; in April 1994 the administrator of the Wage and Hour Division reaffirmed the Labor Department's hope to eliminate the program entirely.

Often acting in concert with the Labor Department, federally funded Legal Services programs have brought blizzards of ideologically motivated suits against hapless orchardists in the program. After enduring two decades of litigation, the Florida sugar industry, traditionally the chief employer of H2A workers, threw in the towel. Jeffrey Ward, counsel to the Sugar Cane Growers Cooperative, says: "Following a freeze, machines may not be able to distinguish between the frozen and unfrozen portions of cane, but they don't sue."

Although opposition to the program rests on the premise that H2A workers depress the wages of domestic workers, in fact the program exerts steady upward pressure on wages.

Congress imposed special requirements on employers who participated in the program. They must first engage in an interstate recruitment effort through the Labor Department, and then must provide transportation, housing, subsidized meals and other benefits to the H2A workers, as well as pay a "prevailing wage rate" fixed by the Labor Department. Once the employer enters the program, he must provide the same benefits to any domestic worker who applies through the first half of the season. Because all this is so expensive, employers tend to bid up wages in the hope of attracting sufficient domestic workers. This in turn pushes up the "prevailing wage rate" each year.

Problems Avoided

The countries that are the source of illegal immigrants much prefer a regularized program, which protects their workers and brings them back each year to invest their dollars in homes and businesses, to the current situation in which their nationals are subject to smugglers, border bandits, employer exploitation, apprehension and deportation. As for this country, a much expanded H2A program would avoid disruption of agriculture, loss of markets loss of complementary jobs filled by U.S. workers (e.g., tractor drivers, packers). And while they create jobs and economic activity that would not otherwise exist, temporary workers do not increase demand for public assistance, education or Social Security.

The House hearings focused on ways to breathe new life into the H2A program so that, like the old bracero program, it can provide agriculture with needed seasonal workers while turning illegal immigration into legal channels. But if the program is to fulfill its promise, Congress must revamp it. Above all, it must take the program out of the hands of the Labor Department and make it off-limits to Legal Services lawsuits.

"We cannot afford any more poor, immigrant farmworkers. Cheap labor is too expensive."

America Should Not Admit Guest Farmworkers

Linda Thom

In the following viewpoint, Linda Thom argues that temporary farmworkers from Mexico should not be brought into California because they would have a negative socioeconomic impact on communities. Thom contends that many such workers and their families would seek to remain in California as illegal immigrants, thus increasing welfare and crime rates. Furthermore, the author maintains, the availability of guest workers would not deter American employers from continuing to hire illegal immigrants. Thom is a budget analyst for the Office of the County Administrator in Santa Barbara, California.

As you read, consider the following questions:

1. What is the hourly wage of strawberry pickers, according to Thom?
2. In Thom's opinion, what allowed producers to grow high-labor-intensive and very profitable crops?
3. What does the author suggest employers do rather than hire guest farmworkers?

Excerpted from Linda Thom, "Do We Really Need Guest Farmworkers?" *Social Contract*, Winter 1995/96. Reprinted with permission.

Editor's note: The following viewpoint is an open letter to California representative Elton Gallegly.

I understand that you support a guest worker program. I hope to convince you that such a proposal is a bad idea for the people you represent in Ventura County. I do not know much about agriculture but I do know a great deal about immigration and its effects on California. The facts are abundant and clear.

Immigrant agricultural workers are poor. Many have moved here with their families and have a significant negative socioeconomic impact on the communities where they work and reside. Your neighboring county to the north, Santa Barbara, is where I live and work. I am a budget analyst in the Office of the Santa Barbara County Administrator. While I do not speak for Santa Barbara County, I do have access to data and I do understand public finance and public programs. This letter contains data on Ventura and Santa Barbara Counties because they have large agricultural industries. Obviously I have more data from Santa Barbara County available to me.

No Shortage of Farmworkers

First, I repeatedly hear that a shortage of farmworkers exists. Perhaps growers in Ventura are telling you that we need a guest worker program because there are not enough farmworkers. There is, in fact, an abundance of farmworkers in Ventura County. Santa Barbara County Job Training Network received a Job Training Partnership Act grant of $511,605. The purpose is to retrain farmworkers for the tri-counties of Ventura, Santa Barbara and San Luis Obispo Counties. The application states in part, "Since IRCA [the Immigration Reform and Control Act] was passed in 1986 the ranks of farmworkers has dramatically increased. . . . The population eligible to receive these benefits [unemployment insurance] is estimated to exceed 76,500 workers [in the tri-counties]."

As the grant is for $511,605 to retrain 84 farmworkers, the cost is $6,091 per worker. To retrain all 76,500 workers in the three counties would, therefore, cost $466 million and that is just three counties in the whole nation. I understand from the Center for Immigration Studies that the Department of Labor has $82 million available nationally to retrain unemployed agricultural workers. If there are 76,500 unemployed farmworkers in three counties and only $82 million to retrain farmworkers for the whole nation, why would we want to add more guest workers to the current oversupply of farm labor helping to insure the continued unemployment of the people who already live here?

As you may know, in Santa Barbara County the majority of

labor-intensive agriculture is in the Santa Maria Valley, and the biggest employers of seasonal labor are the strawberry growers. Currently, broccoli, strawberries, grapes and avocados are Santa Barbara's top crops. All these crops are labor intensive and most of it is seasonal. In an April 1993 survey of growers conducted by the University of California Cooperative Extension Service and published in *Central Coast Agriculture Highlights*, the harvest rates ranged between $4.50 and $5.00 per hour for strawberry pickers. If a worker was employed full time at $5 per hour, his or her annual earnings would be $10,400. These workers are not employed full time, however. They are seasonal.

The article on wages also stated, "More important, growers also indicated the labor problems encountered: 1. high turnover (33%); 2. insubordination (22%); 3. higher unemployment tax rates (22%); 4. absenteeism (17%)." Apparently farmworkers, whether legal or illegal, do not think much of these jobs; nevertheless, Richard Quandt of the Western Grower-Shipper Vegetable Association stated in 1994 in a public forum that illegal aliens comprise 50 percent of the agriculture work force in Santa Maria. Perhaps if wages and work conditions were better, fewer labor problems would occur and fewer illegal aliens would be needed because legal residents would be willing to perform all the available work.

Staying in America

Some suggest that guest workers could solve a labor shortage caused by too few citizens willing to work in agriculture. Guest workers would come from Mexico and then go home after the season ends. The trouble is that they do not go home. Moreover, they bring their families with them. What penalty exists for them if they bring their families? None. A proposal is currently circulating that they would be paid in their home country with the logic that they will have to go home to get their money. With the current porous nature of our borders, what is to keep them and their families from returning? With the economic and political crisis in Mexico, every incentive exists to head north.

Further, why would illegal aliens stop coming and why would they stop bringing their families with them? And why would growers quit hiring illegal aliens? Employers get a 4-percent-of-payroll benefit from hiring illegal workers. How does this happen? Unemployment insurance rates for employers are based on the number of workers who have filed for unemployment. The difference in rates is 4 percent. That is, if an employer has few workers who file claims, then that employer's unemployment insurance rates are 4 percent lower than another employer who has a high incidence of unemployment claims. Illegal aliens are not eligible for unemployment benefits, therefore a laid-off illegal alien does not count against the employer. Of course, this applies to all employers of illegal aliens, not just agricultural employers, but the nature of seasonal agriculture is such that there are many layoffs so this constitutes a significant incentive to hire illegal aliens.

All of these are mere details. The most important factor in the farm labor supply equation is the nature of California agriculture. *Vision 2010: California Agriculture* by the California Department of Food and Agriculture (1990) puts it this way:

> California agriculture has mechanized many tasks . . . but labor demand is still high because acreage of the most labor-intensive crops—fruits, berries, vegetables, and grapes—has been increasing. . . . California agriculture must hire some 900,000 workers each year to bring in its rich harvest of crops. But two thirds of them will do farm work for only a few weeks out of the year. When they are needed, as during the peak summer and fall harvests, they are needed badly. Only about one third have stable, year-round jobs on farms and ranches. Many follow the crops from area to area and state to state. . . . An increasing number have settled down to stay in one area and supplement farm work with what other jobs may be found "

A Labor Surplus

What does this mean? Growers have a large labor surplus made possible by the passage of the 1986 Immigration Reform and Control Act (IRCA) and the continuing flow of illegal aliens across our borders. This labor surplus has made possible the conversion of their crops from low-labor-intensive, less profitable crops to high-labor-intensive, very profitable crops such as strawberries. The low-paying, seasonal jobs and abundant labor supply guarantee poverty among the farmworkers.

And what does "not enough workers" mean? It means that growers want 300 workers for one day, then 500 the next, then after one week, they do not want any at all. When do they want the workers?—when the strawberries need to be picked. When is that? Growers do not know. So what is "enough" in the eyes of the growers? 500 workers, not on the payroll, not in grower-owned housing, waiting around to work on the day the growers want them to work, which may be tomorrow or next week or two weeks from now. Would there be "enough" workers if growers provided housing and wages until the crop is ready to pick? I think so. What would happen if growers converted to less labor-intensive crops which they grew prior to the passage of IRCA? They would make smaller profits. They do not want to do that. They want politicians to guarantee them "enough" cheap, third-world laborers, so they can continue as at present.

What is the price of this? Guaranteeing growers "enough" farmworkers may be good for the growers but the effects on the workers and the local communities are devastating. . . .

Many legal immigrants and illegal aliens are having babies here and as you know well, they are United States citizens at birth. In 1993, 40 percent of Ventura County births were to foreign-born women; 42 percent in Tulare County; 45 percent in Santa Barbara and 50 percent in Monterey County. For the state as a whole, 45 percent of the births were to foreign-born women.

Resist a Guest-Worker Program

By shutting off illegal immigration and resisting the temptations of a new guest-worker program, the nation would force growers to make do with the labor supply that currently exists—and to do whatever it takes to recruit and retain workers. . . .

Illegal immigration is a subsidy for farmers, a subsidy in addition to price supports, marketing arrangements, and cheap water—and another guest-worker program would serve simply to increase this subsidy. What's worse, the distortion of our nation's labor market caused by this subsidy requires further subsidies for legitimate farm workers who are harmed.

Mark Krikorian, *Christian Science Monitor*, July 25, 1995.

If the parents are legal but poor immigrants who have applied for amnesty under IRCA, the family qualifies for Aid to Families with Dependent Children (AFDC). But if the parents are illegal aliens, only the US-born children qualify for AFDC and they are counted in the "child-only" caseload. According to Governor Pete Wilson's Summary Budget for 1994–95, about 10 percent of the child-only cases have caretaker adults who are recipients of Supplementary Security Income (SSI) or they are non-parent relatives. Ninety percent of the child-only cases have parents who are ineligible for aid based on immigration status. The child-only cases between 1985 and 1992 accounted for almost half of California's caseload increase. After 1992, illegal aliens who applied for amnesty started to qualify for AFDC. Recall that they had a waiting period before they could apply. The "experts" said that the number of child-only cases would decline and the number of whole families on assistance would increase. This would only be true if illegal aliens quit coming and having babies. I am sorry to say that the number of IRCA-amnesty families on AFDC has increased, and the number of illegal aliens having babies has increased also, because illegal aliens continue to arrive.

Aid to Families with Dependent Children–Unemployed (AFDC-U) cases are comprised of two-parent families. AFDC–

161

Family Group (AFDC-FG) are single-parent families and these cases account for about 83 percent of the total cases in the state. For agricultural counties, the child-only cases have exploded. The increase is especially large in the AFDC-U caseload but it is also bad in the AFDC-FG caseload. In tracking the AFDC-U, child-only cases in Santa Barbara County, the Spanish-speaking caseload increase is almost identical to the AFDC-U child-only caseload. When graphed, the cases go up and down together and they coincide with the agricultural season. This means that the parents are out of work and they do not qualify for unemployment insurance, but their citizen children qualify for AFDC which is clearly supporting the whole family during the off season. AFDC has become a substitute for unemployment insurance. Employers have to pay for unemployment insurance—the public pays for AFDC. . . .

Swelling Caseloads

Please note, Representative Gallegly, that in Ventura County, the number of AFDC-U, child-only cases comprised 9 percent of the caseload in 1986, and by October 1992 they comprised 32 percent of all cases and made up 61 percent of the increased cases in that period. The AFDC-FG, child-only cases, accounted for 85 percent of the caseload growth. This demonstrates that illegal aliens are here with their families. Why would they go home or quit coming?

The same is true for Santa Barbara County. According to Santa Barbara County Department of Social Services data, between July 1987 and July 1994 the Spanish-speaking, Hispanic AFDC caseload increased from 372 cases to 1,666 cases for a 348 percent increase and accounted for 41 percent of all the AFDC caseload increase in this period.

That is bad enough, but the Medicaid caseload change is worse. Between July 1987 and July 1994, the Spanish-speaking, Hispanic caseload increased from 550 cases to 6,845 cases for a 1,145 percent increase and accounted for 64 percent of all the added cases in this period. In both the AFDC and Medicaid caseload increase, the North County agricultural area increased more than the South County, where low-skilled jobs are mainly in the service industry.

Deplorable Crime Statistics

Representative Gallegly, I know the horse is dead but I am going to beat it one more time. The crime statistics are deplorable. Table 1 shows the change in adult and juvenile felony arrests by race and ethnicity for the period 1986 through 1992. Santa Barbara County data are derived from the California Department of Justice figures.

Table 1. Change in Adult and Juvenile
Felony Arrests by Race and Ethnicity
Santa Barbara County, 1986 to 1992

Adult Arrest Change	White	Hispanic	Black	Other
807	–26	681	149	3
Percent of all change	–3%	84%	18%	0%
Juvenile Arrest Change	White	Hispanic	Black	Other
269	–101	337	20	13
Percent of all change	–38%	125%	7%	5%

Source: California Department of Justice, Criminal Justice Profiles

Crime statistics for the state show generally the same trends except that the category "other," which is mostly Asian/Pacific Islander, shows larger increases in crime in the state because Santa Barbara has a relatively smaller population of Asians compared to the state as a whole.

The *Vision 2010: California Agriculture* report states:

> At present, nothing indicates that California agriculture's need for workers, and for hand labor, will diminish substantially by the year 2010. Not, certainly, if the irrigated high-value specialty crops continue to be so important. . . . It is reasonable to assume, however, that agriculture will face a less abundant supply of labor. Farmers and ranchers may respond to that situation by offering workers better terms of employment. But labor cost is a major expense. California growers are in competition with others around the world who pay far lower wages and far fewer benefits such as pensions and insurance. The question then arises, how far can California growers afford to go in order to assure their labor supply?

Have growers offered workers better terms of employment? No. Instead, growers have convinced many politicians that they need more workers in the form of a guest worker program. If growers must rely on ever increasing sources of third-world labor, what advantage is there to the surrounding communities to subsidize this by picking up the tab in the form of schools overcrowded with impoverished children, increased crime and burgeoning welfare caseloads?

We cannot win a competition for cheap labor with third-world countries. Moreover, this is a race to the bottom that we do not want to win. Let us tell employers to mechanize, convert back to less labor-intensive crops or go out of business. We cannot afford any more poor, immigrant farmworkers.

Cheap labor is too expensive.

Periodical Bibliography

The following articles have been selected to supplement the diverse views presented in this chapter. Addresses are provided for periodicals not indexed in the *Readers' Guide to Periodical Literature*, the *Alternative Press Index*, or the *Social Sciences Index*.

Marc Cooper	"The War Against Illegal Immigrants Heats Up," *Village Voice*, October 4, 1994. Available from 36 Cooper Square, New York, NY 10003.
Sam Dillon	"Border Patrol vs. 'Illegals': And Now, Desert Warfare," *New York Times*, March 26, 1996.
Economist	"Holding the Line," March 16, 1996. Available from PO Box 58524, Boulder, CO 80322-8524.
Mark Krikorian	"To Help Farm Workers, Stop Importing More of Them," *Christian Science Monitor*, July 25, 1995. Available from Reprints, 1 Norway St., Boston, MA 02115.
Howard LaFranchi	"America Puts Up Chain-Links Along a Once-Friendly Border," *Christian Science Monitor*, February 13, 1996.
Howard LaFranchi	"U.S. Border Patrol Sharpens Strategy to Thwart Aliens," *Christian Science Monitor*, February 15, 1996.
Robert W. Lee	"Danger of Government Intrusion," *New American*, February 19, 1996. Available from 770 Westhill Blvd., Appleton, WI 54914.
Migration World	"Immigration Commission Proposals: An Analysis," vol. 22, no. 5, 1994. Available from Center for Migration Studies, 209 Flagg Pl., Staten Island, NY 10304.
José Palafox	"Militarizing the Border," *Covert Action Quarterly*, Spring 1996.
Revolutionary Worker	"The Border War," March 17, 1996. Available from PO Box 3486, Merchandise Mart, Chicago, IL 60654.
Revolutionary Worker	"House Passes Anti-Immigrant Bill," March 31, 1996.
Ann W. Richards	"A Congressional Cure," *Spectrum*, Winter 1994. Available from Council of State Governments, PO Box 11910, Lexington, KY 40578-1910.
Ben Sherwood	"California Leads the Way, Alas," *New York Times*, November 27, 1994.
Julian L. Simon	"Foreign Workers, American Dream," *New York Times*, June 1, 1995.

Are Illegal Immigrants Being Victimized?

Illegal Immigration

Chapter Preface

In August 1995, federal investigators raided an apartment complex in the Los Angeles suburb of El Monte and discovered more than seventy illegal Thai immigrants working in virtual slavery in a garment sweatshop. The workers, who toiled for more than twelve hours daily, were confined behind barbed wire and were rarely allowed outside their cramped quarters.

Immigrant rights activists contend that while the El Monte incident may be an extreme and rare case, illegal immigrants are frequently victims of abuse, discrimination, and exploitation. Many illegal immigrants, activists note, are grossly underpaid, live in poverty, and have few rights. According to Mexican immigrant Roberto Arrelano, U.S. employers of illegal aliens feel "that they can take advantage of undocumented workers, often withholding wages or threatening to reveal us to the Immigration and Naturalization Service."

But opponents of illegal immigration are often less sympathetic and argue that since these immigrants enter the United States illegally, they are not entitled to the same rights and protections as are American citizens and legal immigrants. Thus, critics contend, most complaints about their plight ring hollow. According to educator James Coleman, "Illegal aliens have no right to be treated like Americans. Unless they enter and remain legally, they have no right to our bounty."

Although many Americans sympathize with illegal immigrants who are treated cruelly or unjustly, other citizens maintain that illegal immigrants' status invites discrimination and exploitation and that they should anticipate hardships. The viewpoints in the following chapter debate whether illegal immigrants are being victimized.

VIEWPOINT

1

"[Proposition 187] would open the door to greater discrimination against all those who 'look like immigrants.'"

Anti-Immigrant Sentiment Against Illegal Immigrants Is Unfair

Raúl Hinojosa and Peter Schey

In the following viewpoint, Raúl Hinojosa and Peter Schey argue that proponents of California's Proposition 187, which seeks to deny benefits to illegal immigrants, fuel anti-immigrant sentiment and threaten the well-being of undocumented immigrants. The authors contend that studies exaggerate the economic costs of illegal immigration and do not accurately account for the ways in which illegal immigrants benefit the economy. Hinojosa is the research director of the North American Integration and Development Center at the University of California at Los Angeles. Schey is the executive director of the Center for Human Rights and Constitutional Law in Los Angeles.

As you read, consider the following questions:

1. What do Hinojosa and Schey mean by "manifest destiny"?
2. What percentage of California's Gross State Product is contributed by illegal immigrants, according to Hinojosa and Schey?
3. In the authors' opinion, what types of workers could be required to inform on suspected undocumented residents?

From Raúl Hinojosa and Peter Schey, "The Faulty Logic of the Anti-Immigration Rhetoric," *NACLA Report on the Americas*, vol. 29, no. 3, November/December 1995, pp. 18-22. Copyright 1995 by the North American Congress on Latin America, 475 Riverside Dr., #454, New York, NY 10115-0122. Reprinted with permission.

The upsurge of support in California for Proposition 187 [approved by voters in November 1994], the so-called "Save Our State" ballot initiative, is an ominous manifestation of the fear many U.S. voters have of their future position in a rapidly integrating world economy and an increasingly multicultural society. The Californian economy is undergoing radical changes whose origins lie principally in shifting East-West and North-North relations—the end of the Cold War, the new Pacific economy, and the passage of the GATT [General Agreement on Tariffs and Trade]. Californians, however, have been led by politicians to believe that the state's fiscal crisis is rooted in its North-South relations, particularly its long-term dependence on immigrant labor from Mexico and Central America.

The image of Latin American welfare mothers jumping the border to live off taxpayers and to populate the schools with "illegal" non–English speaking children was too politically potent for Governor Pete Wilson's fledgling and floundering 1994 reelection campaign to pass up. Wilson used Proposition 187 to energize the Republican Party's political base of older white male conservative voters who are openly anxious about the dwindling white majority in the state.

False and Racist Claims

The proposition aspires to transport white voters back to manifest destiny: their God-given right to control and purify the Southwest borderlands. To achieve this, proponents of the measure make the far-fetched claim that the denial of essential services to undocumented immigrants will deter new migrants as well as encourage undocumented residents already in the country to leave voluntarily. The formal argument for the ballot initiative states this mission in militaristic language:

> WE CAN STOP ILLEGAL ALIENS. If the citizens and the taxpayers of our state wait for the politicians in Washington and Sacramento to stop the incredible flow of ILLEGAL ALIENS, California will be in economic and social bankruptcy. We have to act and ACT NOW! On our ballot, Proposition 187 will be the first giant stride in ultimately ending the ILLEGAL ALIEN invasion.

As imitation propositions, bills and campaigns begin to spring up across the country, national and local debates must be made to focus on the wildly false and fundamentally racist claims concerning the economic impact of U.S.-Mexican migration, as well as on the disastrous socioeconomic, transnational and human consequences of any attempt to actually implement these misguided policies. Not only do Prop 187 advocates exaggerate the fiscal costs of immigration, but Mexican-U.S. migrant labor is in fact a major subsidy to California, especially for the prototypical pro-187 voter.

Prop 187 proponents like to point to a series of studies conducted in the early 1990s which concluded that immigration is a burden on taxpayers and a growing part of the state's fiscal crisis. All of these studies share a similar set of suspect estimating techniques concerning the number of undocumented immigrants, the cost of their use of social services, their tax contributions, and the overall economic benefits of Mexican immigration.

First of all, each of these studies can be faulted for its inflated estimates of the number of undocumented immigrants, undocumented children attending schools, and the percentage of these immigrants who are actually deportable by federal law. In his 1994–95 budget, Governor Wilson, for example, stated that there were 2,083,000 undocumented immigrants in California in 1993, including 456,000 undocumented children between the ages of 5 and 17. Interestingly, the Immigration and Naturalization Service (INS), reputed for its excessively high estimates of the nation's undocumented population, reported only 1,441,000 undocumented immigrants in California in October, 1992. Using this estimate and the methodology of California's Department of Finance, one finds that the Governor overestimates by 111,528 (or 24%) the number of undocumented children attending public schools in California. . . .

One of the more sinister methodological tools used in these studies is the creation of a separate accounting category for "Citizen Children of Undocumented Persons." This sort of blood-lineage accounting is not only contrary to the constitutional definition of what constitutes citizenship rights in the United States, but also echoes the kind of fiscal accounting that was used in apartheid South Africa to differentiate the rights of particular legal-ethnic categories.

These anti-immigrant studies then move on to their main mission: producing a cost-benefit analysis with high estimates of the cost of providing social services to undocumented immigrants, and low estimates of local tax revenues collected from this sector of the population.

Taxes and Services

These studies all acknowledge that undocumented immigrants contribute a significant amount in taxes once federal, state and local taxes are added together. California agencies, however, argue that immigrants pay a greater proportion of taxes to the federal government even though local governments are responsible for providing the bulk of social services. What is not mentioned, of course, is that this disproportionate burden upon localities is true for most working-class households in the United States. The real issue is that the federal government has gradually shifted the burden of social-service provision to local governments. Not only is immigration irrelevant to this phenomenon, but according to a 1994 Rand Corporation study, undocumented immigrants actually buffer the effect because they use social services far less than the typical working-class household. This is not surprising given that federal law already renders undocumented immigrants ineligible for most social and health services. Moreover, recent immigrants tend to be healthier than the typical U.S. citizen.

In order to inflate the cost of immigration, Governor Wilson's office added up all current state expenditures (including roads, parks, corporate subsidies, and debt payments), and then calculated the percentage spent on undocumented immigrants and the children of undocumented immigrants based on their share of the population. Notably, if such a formula were used to determine the cost-benefit contribution of all California residents, the gap between what is received from the government and what is contributed in taxes would be wider for U.S. citizens than it is for immigrants.

An Immigrant's Experience of Discrimination

With the discrimination, when I got here, I felt really bad. With my three kids, I was always riding the bus. There was this man who would always look at me and say, "A lot of money." I thought he was saying that I spend a lot of money . . . and I would laugh. Well, no. It was later that I understood that what he was saying was that the government gives me a lot of welfare money for the children. What does that old man know? One has nothing . . . it's there on the bus or on the Metro . . . ayye . . . and how those people look at me. It's as if they're going to bite me, it makes me mad. Just because they see me there with kids.

And I go and do cleaning on Saturdays (cleaning offices) and I took my son, and this one person who was getting on the bus she did like this [making a gesture of disgust] as if they didn't like that we were there. And then my kid asked me: "Mommy, why did that lady do that?" I said, "Just forget it, don't pay attention to her." I don't know who they think they are. It's discrimination.

Isabel, quoted by *Revolutionary Worker*, March 10, 1996.

In a particularly egregious, but oft-cited 1993 study, Donald Huddle of Rice University ignores the money that immigrants give to the government in the form of social-security taxes, unemployment insurance, vehicle-registration fees, and state and federal gasoline taxes. These taxes total $28.8 billion on a national scale. Huddle makes an additional $21.3 billion accounting error by underestimating the income of legal immigrants and using inaccurate tax rates. As an Urban Institute study points out, Huddle's underestimation of revenue from immigrants by $50 billion more than offsets his total annual "net cost" of $42.5 billion. The Rand study drives this point home. It found that the annual taxes paid by immigrants to all levels of government total $25 to $30 billion more than the costs of services they receive.

These immigration studies also systematically underestimate or ignore the diverse ways that immigrants contribute to the U.S. economy apart from the payment of taxes. The studies don't, for example, take into account the economic benefits of immigrant-owned business or the national wealth generated by consumer spending by immigrants. Moreover, they ignore the taxable goods and services that immigrant labor creates. . . .

Illegal Immigrants' Contributions

Undocumented immigrants contribute roughly 7% of the state's $900 billion Gross State Product. Large parts of California's economy—in particular agriculture and the garment industry—would simply not be viable without undocumented workers. The fact that undocumented immigrants are paid on average 15 to 20% less for comparable work generates significant price subsidies for the consumers of the goods and services which immigrants provide.

Some of the largest consumers of immigrant low-cost services are, ironically, typical pro-187 voters: older white property owners with high levels of disposable income to spend on gardeners, nannies and housecleaners. Job competition between undocumented immigrants and the bulk of pro-187 voters is virtually non-existent. By contrast, there is evidence of competition with other Latino legal residents, the majority of whom voted against the proposition.

If we begin to calculate exactly who owes whom for the social reproduction of this low-wage labor force, it is indisputable that the government of California is heavily indebted to Mexico—not the reverse. Mexico spends $180 million annually to educate Mexicans who then migrate without documents to the United States for their prime working years. If one factored in how much Mexico spends on medical services, housing, and urban infrastructure, the amount that California owes Mexico would grow even larger. This represents a fantastic bargain for Governor Wilson because to educate these same workers in California would cost $3.2 billion a year. This is more than double the amount that the Governor complains that the state spends on educating undocumented immigrants. . . .

The overall long-term impact of Prop 187 on Californian society would be negative in a variety of ways. First of all, public health would be seriously compromised. Pregnant women would be denied prenatal care while children who have been abused or neglected would not receive social services. Undocumented residents with serious illnesses would be denied needed medical attention. Others, fearing deportation, would be deterred from seeking medical care when sick. Communicable diseases would spread, endangering the health of all Californians.

Medical experts point out that the cost of health care would skyrocket under Prop 187 since health workers are mandated to provide expensive emergency services that could have been avoided by far less costly early intervention. The Chief of Staff of the Los Angeles County Medical Center, the largest public hospital in California, predicts that while Proposition 187 may save the state about $9 million annually, the costs for emergency care as well as for the treatment of U.S. citizens with communicable diseases will rise by $47 million, resulting in net costs of over $38 million.

Proposition 187 would also bar undocumented children from attending public schools. Testimonials from teachers and educators throughout the country speak of the irreparable harm this would cause these children. Since most undocumented children eventually become lawful permanent residents, and later U.S. citizens, the long-term costs to California of implementing Prop 187 are enormous. These youngsters would become largely unemployable, rely extensively on public-support programs, and be more likely to turn to crime to support themselves.

If implemented, Prop 187 will also move California well along the road towards a police state. The measure mandates a vast state network of informants. Employees of schools, medical clinics, social-service agencies, and state and local law-enforcement agencies would all be required to ferret out suspected undocumented residents and report them to the INS and the Justice Department. Of course, none of these people have the training to make such determinations. This would open the door to greater discrimination against all those who "look like immigrants."

"There is nothing quiet about the individuals who are feverishly working to destroy America as a Western civilization—with our tax dollars."

Anti-Immigrant Sentiment Against Illegal Immigrants Is Justified

Ruth Coffey

In the following viewpoint, Ruth Coffey asserts that illegal immigrants—and individuals who seek to include them in society—are destroying America's identity. Coffey objects that laws and standards are being violated to facilitate illegal immigrants' presence in America and to encourage immigrants to retain their language and culture rather than assimilate into U.S. society. Consequently, she contends, the criteria for becoming a U.S. citizen have been weakened considerably. Coffey, a columnist for the *National Times* monthly magazine, is the president of Stop Immigration Now, a Long Beach, California, organization that seeks to reduce immigration to America.

As you read, consider the following questions:

1. What is the goal of people who wish to abolish the Immigration and Naturalization Service, in Coffey's opinion?
2. In the author's opinion, of what type of Americans is Zoë Baird an example?
3. What is the purpose of a plan to send Mexican teachers to U.S. public schools, according to Coffey?

Excerpted from Ruth Coffey, "Notes from the Immigration Front," *Chronicles: A Magazine of American Culture*, December 1993. Reprinted by permission of the author.

In less than two generations, America has evolved from a nation of proud, courageous, freedom-loving citizens into a fragmented group of pandering, cowardly supplicants who spend their days pleading with ethnic "political piranhas" and their advocates in the media to forgive them for taking up space in their own country, speaking their own language, cherishing their own traditions and history, and, above all, having the temerity to ask that the laws of this land be obeyed. Proof that we are no longer a country of red-blooded Americans who brook no interference from any foreign country was the news report of a March 8, 1993, "hearing" held at Fort Mason, California, to collect testimony from "immigrant" (translate, "illegal alien") women claiming to be the victims of everything from rape to inadequate wages.

Coordinated by organizations with names like the Coalition for Immigrant and Refugee Rights and Services (and its Women's Task Force), Equal Rights Advocates, and the Legal Aid Society of San Mateo County, this illegal alien get-together was championed by such people as Elissevet Stamatopoulou, Chief of the United Nations Center for Human Rights, who was quoted as saying, "[W]e have to shake things up." At age 67, I can remember a time when someone like this U.N. interloper would have been first punched in the nose and then run out of town for daring to dictate the laws of this country to its citizens or to defend the people who contemptuously break them. . . .

The Push for Open Borders

What's more terrifying than the fact that American citizens seem to have had their courage and loyalty sucked up by a giant political vacuum cleaner is that they are not even aware of what is really behind such "human rights hearings" for illegal aliens. Simply put, there has been a concerted attempt by those with a vested interest in opening our country's borders to abolish the INS [Immigration and Naturalization Service] as a law enforcement agency and to utilize its personnel to expedite the relocation of *more* immigrants to this country. The next step will naturally be to disband the border patrol completely, since we will have no use for it with open borders.

If anyone views these comments with skepticism, I suggest he get hold of a copy of the October 26, 1992, *Los Angeles Times* and read an editorial entitled "Bush vs. Clinton: What Would Be the Best Immigration Policy?" This article describes how a "border-effort" consolidation would merge all of our immigration agencies into one and "focus more resources and attention on helping immigrants assimilate into U.S. life."

The editorial also tells of "another good idea quietly working its way through government policy circles in Mexico City" that would have *Mexico* helping the United States regulate the flow of Mexican workers into this country. Yet there is nothing quiet about the individuals who are feverishly working to destroy America as a Western civilization—with our tax dollars. . . . America is joining the ranks of those countries whose conquered citizens strew flowers beneath the feet of their invaders.

Employing Illegals

As one of the countless thousands of American citizens who vehemently opposed Zoë Baird's 1993 appointment to the office of U.S. Attorney General, I too was highly gratified to find that our righteous protests were successful. Yet unlike most of those citizens who bombarded the switchboards and FAX machines of our capital to vent outrage at an individual who had brazenly violated our nation's immigration laws, I was not ready for a victory parade since I realized that Baird's rejection was just one small battle in the prolonged war against the growing invasion of illegal aliens and against those like Baird who aid and abet their presence in our country. [Baird had once employed two illegal immigrants as domestic workers.]

As a matter of fact, news of Baird's rejection wasn't even official before I had begun to find out how and why the employment agencies that recruit illegal aliens for American employers are allowed to profit from violating our country's immigration laws. First, I contacted the agent in charge of the Hartford, Connecticut, Immigration and Naturalization Service and asked what steps, if any, had been taken to investigate the two employment agencies there that had been mentioned in the press as suppliers of illegal alien help. The answer: "Nothing." The explanation? "There are only six INS agents in Connecticut to oversee a population of three-and-a-half million."

Then I contacted the office of California State Senator Quentin Kopp (an outspoken opponent of illegal immigration) and requested his help in alerting the California State Labor Board (which licenses employment agencies) and the INS to the fact that California has numerous businesses that solicit illegal aliens as employees for affluent residents. I also asked that he immediately initiate an investigation of such businesses and that he encourage enforcement of employer sanction laws. For those of you unfamiliar with these laws, they are part of the 1986 Immigration Act, which declared amnesty for all illegal aliens who could prove continuous residence in the United States since before 1982, as well as meet certain other minimum requirements. This legislation entitled millions of illegal aliens to a "green card," or work permit, which allowed them to work in this country indefinitely. It also subjected employers who hired immigrants without this legal proof of residency to varying fines.

Yet in spite of this law, the hiring of illegal aliens continues unabated. Patty Siegel, executive director of the California Child Care Resources and Referral Network, estimates that among California families with children under one year old where both parents are working professionals more than one-third rely on illegal aliens for their child care. In Los Angeles, by some estimates, 80 percent of all domestics are hired illegally. And, as the *Los Angeles Times* reported in January 1993, INS largely allows such practices to go unchallenged. What we witnessed in the case of Zoë Baird was just a skirmish. The switchboards and FAX machines of our elected officials function every day: we must bombard them until the war against the invaders of our country (and those who assist them) is won.

A Mockery of Citizenship

Contrary to the popular belief that illegal aliens must become proficient in English, possess a general knowledge of our nation's history, and understand government procedure to qualify for permanent residency, all that our amnesty program (a result of the 1986 Immigration Act) required until recently was that applicants attend certain "approved" classes for a minimum of 40 hours. Ask the average American what the amnesty program is and undoubtedly he will reply that it is funded by the federal government for the purpose of educating illegal aliens so that they can meet the qualifications for residency or citizenship. But nothing could be further from the truth.

For those illegal aliens who can't (sometimes after more than 15 years of residency) answer, orally and in English, nine out of 15 questions (such as "Which office deals with immigration: the INS, the employment office, the social security office, or the post office?") there was an even more simplified method of attaining the status of permanent resident. According to the January 29, 1989, issue of the *Los Angeles Herald Examiner*, for those illegal aliens who had not miraculously developed a burning desire to become citizens, speak English, or learn American history, but wanted merely to avoid deportation, the amnesty program created an alternative. With this method, all that amnesty applicants were required to do was to show up for at least 40 hours of a 60-hour civics course. Upon fulfillment of this requirement, applicants were awarded certificates of attendance that automatically rendered them eligible for permanent residency.

For the most part, "instructors" in the "learning centers" providing the 60-hour course comprised those quick to jump on a gravy boat kept afloat with billions of federal tax dollars. Since the amnesty program provided for up to 190 hours of free "tutoring" to each illegal alien, these instructors were also quick to encourage their pupils to extend their classroom time from the minimum 40 hours to an average of 150 hours. Because instructors were paid for each hour a pupil spent in the "learning centers," it doesn't take a computer to figure out that transforming illegal aliens into legal aliens was a lucrative business. (One Los Angeles school had an enrollment of more than 3,000 pupils.) In fact, in 1989 California demanded $50 million in addition to the $354.1 million over five years already allotted the state for this program. While the last aliens to go through the amnesty program were to complete their courses by November 1990, this might well be the start of a vicious cycle whereby taxpayers periodically fund the transformation of illegal immigrants into "permanent residents."

Ridiculously Easy

All this is in no way meant to imply that out of the millions of aliens who took advantage of the amnesty program to become legal, a small percentage won't ultimately apply for (and acquire) citizenship after the required five-year wait. The very fact that a modestly intelligent ten-year-old could pass the qualifying test makes citizenship ridiculously easy to attain for anyone with a vocabulary of a few hundred English words and the ability to memorize the answers to a few simple questions.

In fact, as a result of the Immigration Act of 1990, it is now possible to become a citizen by mail. Before, new citizens had to attend a formal naturalization ceremony before a judge, in which they took an oath of loyalty to the flag, Constitution, and laws of the United States. Now, citizenship papers are mailed to our country's new "citizens" upon request. Or, as in Tucson, Arizona, in 1993, Hispanic immigrants are welcomed to American citizenship *in Spanish*. Organized by Tucson's INS office, which thought conducting citizenship ceremonies in a foreign language would be a "nice gesture" to recent immigrants, the city's program demanded only that the oath of loyalty be recited in English (as required by law).

Seeking Political Power

There is no longer any difference between an American "citizen" and a "naturalized" voter. Latino and other ethnic organizations (like the National Association of Latino Elected and Appointed Officials) are feverishly engaged in setting up "learning centers" of their own, in which "their people" are instructed in how to apply for citizenship—and thus attain "political power." Power over *whom* is not entirely clear, but the implication is that they wish to lord it over citizens of the country that offered them hospitality and freedom to begin with.

In none of the thousands of articles I have read or the endless harangues I have heard from the leaders of organizations with names like the Mexican American Legal Defense and Education

Fund (MALDEF), the National Council of La Raza ("The Race"), and the League of Latin American Citizens (LULAC) has the word "privilege" been used in connection with the concept of American citizenship. Nor have I heard anyone explain that citizenship consists of more than rushing off to the voting booth to elect the candidate of one's choice—or rather of the aforementioned ethnic organizations' choice. Hermandad Mexicana Nacional, an affiliate of La Raza deemed eligible by the INS to administer American citizenship examinations, actually incited Mexicans in California to *break* the laws of this country. In the summer of 1992, the Hermandad—or "Brotherhood" (which reportedly received $8.3 million in federal grants for "educational programs" in 1991–1992)—organized a strike of drywall workers, which involved numerous illegal aliens and which resulted in violent scufflings with police officers on more than one occasion.

America's Illegal Immigrant Population, 1994

Overstayed Visas	Source	Entered Illegally
357,000	Mexico	1,199,000
25,000	El Salvador	360,000
53,000	Guatemala	99,000
78,000	Canada	36,000
107,000	Poland	1,000
106,000	Philippines	—
102,000	Haiti	2,000
84,000	Bahamas	—
15,000	Nicaragua	65,000
79,000	Italy	—
1,064,000	Others	147,000
2,070,000	TOTAL	1,909,000

Source: United States Immigration and Naturalization Service

To these organizations, and to all the apathetic American citizens who continue to ignore their bid for ethnic dictatorship, I offer the words of James Baldwin: "The making of an American begins at that point where he himself rejects all other ties, any other history, and himself adopts the vesture of his adopted land." This should be required reading for every elected official and for every individual responsible for reducing the requirements for citizenship and voter registration to no more than an inconvenient formality.

Mexican Teachers in U.S. Schools

The January 19, 1993, issue of the *San Diego Union* laid out details of a mind-boggling plan to send *Mexican* teachers into *our* country's tax-funded public schools to instruct Mexican students in the history and culture of Mexico. This comes at a time when *American* teachers in California have had to agree to a devastating salary cut in order to keep *their* jobs, yet the plan has to date gone unchallenged.

While dedicated American citizens are working tirelessly to secure our country's borders against the invasion of millions of illegal aliens, our school and civic leaders have been making plans to give Mexico carte blanche to run this country's schools by remote control. Actually, there is nothing "remote" about permitting Mexican teachers with Mexican textbooks to teach (in Spanish) Mexican history, Mexican culture, and, for all I know, Mexican cooking to teenage Mexican students in taxpayer-funded American classrooms: sponsored by the Mexican Ministry of Education, the San Diego program includes esteem-building talks by psychologists and professors so teens can "value themselves and their rich culture" and learn that "to be Mexican is not to be bad, not to be stupid."

There is also nothing remote about the possibility that a large number of these Mexican students are *illegal aliens*. Nor is there anything remote about the possibility that, since the Mexican instructors will be responsible for determining who qualifies for a high-school equivalency diploma, all students will be promptly registered as voters. For if California Assemblyman Joe Baca is successful in having his proposed legislation enacted, all California students 18 years or older will be registered to vote as part of their U.S. government and civics courses.

This insidious plan on the part of the Mexican government and its American allies to indoctrinate Mexican expatriates in undying loyalty to the country from which they so willingly fled is unconscionable as well as of dubious constitutionality: the Mexican government has admitted its political motives behind the adult and teen education programs, citing concern about the number of Mexican immigrants in the United States still voting at home and influencing events there.

179

"I used to cry, I used to become so desperate because I couldn't find the door out of this situation."

Undocumented Workers Are Exploited

Revolutionary Worker

Government officials suspect that some 10 percent of more than one hundred thousand garment workers in Los Angeles are undocumented immigrants. In the following viewpoint, Valentina—a previously undocumented garment worker and a single mother of two sons—reveals to the *Revolutionary Worker* her struggles to make ends meet by working in the underground garment industry. Valentina argues that because illegal immigrants cannot ask U.S. government agencies for help, they have no choice but to work long hours for low wages. The *Revolutionary Worker* is a publication of the Revolutionary Communist Party.

As you read, consider the following questions:

1. What was the "double problem" that Valentina and similar women faced, according to the *Revolutionary Worker*?
2. According to Valentina, how much was her piece-rate payment per garment?
3. From where does Valentina contend she found strength?

"The Story of Valentina," *Revolutionary Worker*, November 26, 1995. Reprinted by permission of the *Revolutionary Worker*, the weekly newspaper of the Revolutionary Communist Party, U.S.A. Greenhaven editors have retitled and added some subheadings and a boxed quotation to the original article.

Valentina arrived in Los Angeles 15 years ago. Since then she has attained residency for herself and her children. Yet residency has not shielded her or provided the protection from being exploited as a worker or from women's oppression. Not from the garment shop owners or men who seek to dominate women.

On the contrary. As a worker, her labor has produced thousands upon thousands of clothes, yet she can barely purchase back the clothes for her son. As a woman alone with kids, it has made her the object of super exploitation and wages of hunger, working at home doing double work taking care of her home and family and earning a living.

Valentina is one of these strong sisters. When she talks to you, she looks at you straight in the eye and says what's on her mind. She has an easy smile and contagious laughter. She lives in a one-bedroom apartment with one of her two sons. The other has grown up and has moved out.

Valentina has recently started a new job in a garment shop. But these last eight years she has spent behind a sewing machine at home, working for *La Costura* [a large Los Angeles garment manufacturing center].

Her apartment is neatly kept. The place is tiny, the living room and the kitchen are occupied by two sewing machines. On one wall there are photographs of her children and what appears to be her family in Mexico. There is a radio and a television set, some chairs and a table.

We sit in her kitchen to talk. Valentina's attention seems to be divided between several things happening at the same time: There is the food on the stove, there are children playing outside, her son comes in and out of the apartment, he is recording some rap tunes on the radio and hanging out with his friends. Valentina keeps an eye on all these things as we talk, yet she doesn't skip a beat.

"I am from XX [a town in Mexico], and from there I have had very bad luck with my husband, my children's father. Back there in XX, it's a 'rancho'—women do not go out to work. You do the cooking, housework, but not other kinds of work. Women don't even go into the fields. So I came here because I had a child and I no longer belonged to my parents' home, because I was already married."

On Her Own

"I separated from my husband, and I went to my parents, and my parents said, 'You have to do something and it will have to be you by yourself. You'll have to go away or who knows what, so that you can bring up your child.'

"So I was 18 years old when I got to Tijuana. There in TJ I worked in a home and also in fashions, fashions like wedding dresses. Back in those days, I would earn $20 a week. When I was working in the homes, I earned $8 a week. I am talking about 15 years ago. In those days, the food was cheap.

"I was living in an apartment by myself, I was paying $35 for the place. And that was how I began to fend for myself. Then, the dollar began to go up and up and up. It wreaked chaos, everything got expensive. So I said to myself, the dollar is up and here things are expensive, and because of this it was necessary to come over to the U.S.

"I crossed the border, I came across the hills. It was dangerous, I crossed four times. And I was caught four times. Two times I was held one week by immigration because I had been caught several times before. So it was like that until I made it over.

Exploitation by Garment Manufacturers

The garment manufacturers cited for violations of safety and labor laws usually have employed immigrants, men and women sometimes unfamiliar with U.S. law or desperate to earn even meager wages. For all our praise of America as a land of immigrants, exploitation of newcomers has been a too-frequent phenomenon. The terrible conditions of the garment sweatshops on New York City's Lower East Side at the start of the 1900s should be matter for the history books. They should not be replicated at the end of the century.

Los Angeles Times, February 20, 1996.

"Finally I arrived in Los Angeles. I was alone with my child, I suffered a lot. It was this dark sadness. At first, I lived with this lady and she would tell me: 'You have to pay me $250 a month.' Ooh my god! why so much money?! Then she would come around again asking for another $50, and I was only earning $140. But I had to pay $250 a month—and that was so I could sleep on the living room floor with my child.

"When I first got to Los Angeles, I did not know how to run a machine, because the machines are different, they are industrial machines, they are heavy duty. I learned in this garment shop, there they taught me. One starts by the easiest and that is on the standard machine that sews straight.

"Now I have about 15 years working in garment. Little by little one goes gaining experience, one gets cuffs to do, then the collars, zippers. There are different materials—some are more difficult to sew, like silk and satin. A man's shirt is simple. All the materials that are thin and delicate is difficult to work.

"The pay is the lowest, the least they can pay you. For example, if I am working in a company and they only give me hems to do, I have to make a lot of pieces. If they pay at ten cents or at eight or at five cents a piece, I have to move fast to earn $30 to $40 a day. Really killing myself, wearing myself out."

A Double Burden

Like many single mothers, Valentina was faced with a double problem shared by millions of women. Somehow she needed to survive and take care of her children. One option was to find another husband to help with the costs of living—an arrangement of convenience. This was a particularly distasteful option to Valentina. She is a woman who is not willing to be dominated or brutalized. She thinks that among couples there has to be equality and mutual respect. Valentina comments that:

"A woman in this country has to be much stronger than the man. She has to be strong and she also has to be able to overcome obstacles on her own without a husband. All my life, I have been alone. I never had a husband. I was married, but that was no good for me. On my own, I've had to persevere. I am of the opinion that a woman may have to work like hell, but something's got to come out of it, something's got to change."

The other "option" that presented itself was the "opportunity" to work at home sewing for a sweatshop. The "opportunity" presented itself when a shopowner "facilitated" the acquisition of a sewing machine and the delivery of work to Valentina's home. It was an "opportunity" to work as a slave, the "facility" to be entombed, isolated, working from sun-up till late night, seven days a week, buried under garments in her apartment alone for the next eight years. Valentina explains:

"Well, I work at home because I had to take care of my children. The little one is in school, the older one now works but before I had to fix him his food.

"Getting a machine in your home depends on the agreement you may have with your boss. That machine he facilitated it for me, the payments and all. I bought it new for $840 and I paid it off to him in three payments of $300 each in three months. He would discount this from my check when he brought the work to me.

Piece-Rate Work

"I have worked here in my house, alone. So I would rush to get the money I needed, really killing myself, wearing myself out. From 5 or 6 in the morning till 10 or 11 at night—all day working and part of the night, all week, Saturdays and Sundays, I never took a rest.

"I would get paid at piece rate. For piece rate, I was getting 90 cents and 60 cents for an *entire garment*. So for me to get $600 or

$800 I had to work an entire month, nonstop.

"Sometimes I would make 600 shirts in a month, sometimes 800. But that was *no eight-hour day.* I had to put in a lot more hours than that. Then, the shirt would cost you $26 in a store, and I would get 90 cents for making it.

"Everything was done over the phone, I would call my boss and tell him, 'I did this much and for that much,' and he would say, 'OK, I'll make out your check,' and he would come by for the tickets.

"How do you keep track of your pay? It's with tickets. Each bundle has a ticket, if the ticket has 30 pieces for 90 cents then I would use my calculator and figure it out, then on the phone I would talk to the boss. He would come for the tickets, give me my paycheck and bring me more work.

"If the machine broke down, I had to fix it, or call a mechanic. The mechanic charges $25 to $30 for the time he fixes the machine. I pay for the needles on the machine, the belts, oiling it, spare parts, the electricity, everything. The factory only gives me the thread.

"I was like that for eight years. Here locked up in my house. What kept me going all that time? I had two things on my mind. My children and work. I had to juggle everything. I had to take care of my home and I had to work. For women it's double work, taking care of my kids, cooking . . . cleaning house . . . everything, *everything!*

Balancing Work and Family

"A mom is always looking for a way to solve the problems. And it is so true—women work more because after working eight hours, many women come home to cook dinner, they come home tired. When my kids came home, my kids could see how tired I was, but they are waiting for me—waiting for me to make them food. One of my kids is learning how to cook, but the other hasn't learned yet. Before, I used to cry, I used to become so desperate because I couldn't find the door out of this situation.

"Every morning I would get up and sew. I would go straight to the machine. My kid would get up at 6:30 a.m., get himself ready and go to school. I would stay home and work. At 11 I would stop to have lunch, at 2:30 he would come home, by then I would prepare dinner, then I would continue working. I don't know how I did it all that time. It was only work and I would never go outside.

"I usually shop on the weekends—I don't go to the markets during the week. And the only other time I would go out would be to pay the bills. I walk two blocks to the station, but that would just take me an hour. But then again, I would have to report to work that I was leaving my house when I had to go pay my bills.

"My boss didn't want the job to stop. He wanted the work done as fast as possible. And he would tell me: 'I got you on social security and time is running for every hour' that I was working. But the hours that I wouldn't work to go pay my bills, I wasn't getting paid. So I don't understand what he was talking about. I would only get paid for the pieces done. It was like a contract. If I would get a thousand shirts, and if he wanted it done in a month, then I have to hurry myself, work day and night so I would not look bad in his eyes. Particularly towards the end, there was so much pressure. He wanted control. Finally he said to me, 'I can't be helping you no more.' I wasn't able to produce enough for him. So I had to find work somewhere else."

From Homework to Sweatshop

Valentina has found another job in garment, making samples—no longer production or piece rate, no longer working at home. While on the one hand she tells me that she is doing fine now, having left behind a nightmare, the beginning of a new round has begun, working in a garment factory. She explains:

"I have already gone through those times, and it was very difficult for me. I believe that there is people right now that are going through that. Right now there are a lot of us mothers who are going through the same thing. But, every woman has a different story. Now that my 'baby' is grown, life is not so hard. Right now the problem I have is that to support him with clothes and shoes, and then rent, along with the bills, money is still not enough. And sometimes I try and think, why is the money not enough, now that I am making good money? I don't know what goes on.

"Everything here is too expensive. I believe that in five more years I will not be able to work.

"Where do I find the strength? I believe it comes from oneself, because if the woman does not become strong, then who will make her strong? No one! In this country people don't give a helping hand to each other. Here no one knows you. *No one!* You live in apartments, but you don't know the name of the one upstairs, you don't know the name of the people next door.

Whatever It Takes

"A woman that is alone who has children, what can she do? *You tell me!* What can she do?—Work! Do whatever it takes to care for her kids. A woman who is not born here, a woman who has no papers, she can't ask the government anything. Why? Because she don't have the documents they ask for—the requirements that they have. So, she has to work, and work hard, hard, *hard!* so that she can move up from under.

185

"Many thousands [of illegal immigrants] . . . eventually surface to pay taxes, gain legal status and achieve their goals."

Undocumented Workers Can Find Prosperity

Evelyn Nieves

In the following viewpoint, Evelyn Nieves reports on the Vasquezes, a Panamanian couple with three children, who arrived in the United States with tourist visas and remained illegally. Nieves describes the Vasquezes' endeavor—from 1984 through the early 1990s—to find jobs, improve their English skills, and acquire legal documents to achieve a better life in America. Nieves writes that after years of saving money, the Vasquezes purchased a home and were close to becoming legal residents. Nieves is a *New York Times* staff writer.

As you read, consider the following questions:

1. Why did Yolanda Vasquez seek work as a maid, according to Nieves?
2. According to the author, how much do the Vasquezes earn annually?
3. What type of business does Mr. Vasquez hope to start, according to Nieves?

Evelyn Nieves, "Newcomers Find Success Despite Barriers," *New York Times*, June 18, 1993. Copyright 1993 by The New York Times Company. Reprinted by permission.

After following their dreams to the United States, Yolanda Vasquez and her husband found themselves in a dark, three-room tenement in North Bergen, New Jersey, with a mattress on the floor, wondering what had possessed them to leave Panama.

They had no working papers, no job connections and few prospects—at a time when immigration laws were about to become stricter and halfway decent jobs hard to come by, even for Americans

But now, like many thousands of other immigrants who make their way against great odds, they are on the verge of success. After nearly nine years in the United States, they already own a three-bedroom ranch on a cul-de-sac, spend most weekends chauffeuring their three children to soccer matches and hold two individual retirement accounts. Any day now, they will also be legal residents.

The journey this couple made—starting out in the region's underground economy—does not always end in success. The underground economy—a world that is off the books and unregulated—has virtually enslaved thousands of vulnerable immigrants, exploiting their desperation by forcing them into the worst jobs for the worst pay.

But it has also served to sustain and nurture many thousands more who eventually surface to pay taxes, gain legal status and achieve their goals.

Experts say that those most likely to succeed are much like Ms. Vasquez and her husband, who were both well educated when they got here and had the advantage of a relative already living legally in this country.

Not Without Hardship

But theirs was not a journey without hardship. For this couple, it has involved one route for the husband and one for the wife. He worked 12-hour days, seven days a week, for years. She had to work as a live-in maid, hostage to a job she hated, because she knew that maids, sponsored by their employers, are almost guaranteed they will be granted legal status. The children, two boys, 14 and 12, and a daughter, 13, suffered too. Often lonely in a strange land, they spent long hours with baby-sitters and many hours by themselves as their parents worked to establish themselves.

Sitting on a rose chintz sofa in their living room on a Sunday afternoon, the couple talked of how far they had come even without a green card. They love the security and convenience of their Brick Township neighborhood, a sleepy block of identical houses on quarter-acre lots bordering several large roadside malls and plazas. Both have become fluent in English; Ms. Vasquez barely has an accent. Together, they make $55,000 a year, with $45,000 coming from wages and overtime earned by Ms. Vasquez's husband.

"Now, getting all the papers means we have arrived," said Ms. Vasquez, who is 41 years old. "But, whew!" She pretended to wipe sweat from her brow. "It has been very hard."

Ms. Vasquez's husband, who is 39 and came to New York on a tourist visa in 1984, one year before the rest of the family, expects his green card, or permanent visa, soon. Because he is not a legal resident yet, he spoke only on the condition that he not be identified in order to protect his job as a manager in a parking garage in northern New Jersey. Ms. Vasquez, who usually uses her husband's last name, would only allow her given surname to be used. She and the children received permanent visas in 1992, after applying when Ms. Vasquez began working as a maid in 1985.

A Simple Plan

When Ms. Vasquez's husband came to New York, the plan was so simple: Get a high-paying job, save money, and send for the family. He believed that a job—any job—was the ticket to becoming a permanent resident of the United States.

He had decided to come after constant prodding from his brother-in-law, a native Colombian who is a naturalized American citizen, and his sister.

The couple lived in David, the capitol of Chiriqui, on Panama's west coast, where they both had good jobs. He headed the human resources department of a major company. She was a social worker. But they came to believe that their children, who were still preschoolers, would never have the same educational opportunities as their American counterparts.

"Panama doesn't have the technology," Ms. Vasquez's husband explained.

When he arrived in New York, in 1984, Ms. Vasquez's husband stayed with his sister and brother-in-law in Astoria [Queens, New York] while he began looking for work by scouring the want ads in the Sunday papers. But he knew little English beyond "How are you?" "I am fine, thank you." No job fit the bill for a manager/accountant who couldn't speak the language.

Rough Times at Work

Meanwhile his sister and brother-in-law told him to apply for a New York State driver's license. All it took, he said, was a written test at the Department of Motor Vehicles and proof from the Panamanian consulate that he had been a licensed driver in Panama.

By his second month here, his brother-in-law also got him a Social Security number and card—sold by its owner—from an acquaintance in Astoria with connections in the underground economy.

"I didn't know that it belonged to somebody," Ms. Vasquez's husband said of the card. "I didn't know what an illegal alien was. All I knew was that I was told I needed the card to work."

Software Entrepreneurs

Many of the largest and most important technology companies of the 1980s in California and elsewhere were created by immigrants, including Sun Microsystems, AST, ALR, Applied Materials, Everex, and Gupta. Borland International, a premier software company worth hundreds of millions of dollars, was founded by Philippe Kahn, an illegal immigrant.

Ron K. Unz, *Reason*, November 1994.

Actually, at first he didn't need the card. His first three jobs, brokered by an employment agency he found in the classifieds of *Noticias del Mundo*, a Spanish-language newspaper, were in places employing illegal immigrants. He was dismissed from the first, a midtown croissant shop, after two hours for failing to understand a sandwich order. He quit the second, as a delivery-man for a Times Square diner, after getting paid $60 for a 60-hour week. (He had been promised $130.) At the third, a Greek diner in Queens, he dropped a tray in the dining room, sending plates and glasses crashing "with tremendous noise." The owner paid him $80 for four days of work and said he would get a call if the diner needed him.

Making a Living

It took close to six months to find a steady job, at a parking garage under a midtown hotel. When the employers asked him for a driver's license and Social Security card, he was able to show both.

By this time, his visa had expired. He and his brother-in-law went to an immigration lawyer in Queens for help and were told that to get a visa he needed the kind of job that would lead an employer to sponsor his application. Live-in domestic work qualified. Parking cars did not.

But the garage paid relatively well—$4 an hour when the minimum wage was $3.35—and he decided to stay there. He set aside the issue of his residency and began taking English classes twice a week for $60 a week at a midtown language center,

He also opened a savings account at a Queens bank. And he received his first credit card, by applying for a $500 credit limit, the minimum the bank offered.

Two months after he started working at the garage, he was ready to bring the family over.

Moving to New Jersey

Ms. Vasquez and the children arrived in New York on tourist visas to find their new home was a two-story clapboard building on North Bergen's busiest commercial strip. On the advice of a co-worker, Ms. Vasquez's husband had crossed the Hudson River to find an affordable apartment. The rent: $500 a month.

"It was not a very nice apartment," he said.

But they could save money. A month later, they bought their first car, a 1978 Ford Fairlane, for $1,300.

They planned to have Ms. Vasquez's college transcripts transferred here so that she could get a job as a social worker and apply for a green card. Meanwhile, she enrolled in Hudson County Community College where she took six credits in English and social service. "We considered it an investment," Ms. Vasquez said.

"It was a happy time," her husband said. "We started to travel around. One of the first places we took them to was Washington, D.C. I learned how to use a map. We went to Vermont. We went to Great Adventure."

Ms. Vasquez began applying for county social-service jobs but was told she needed to learn more English.

"The plan wasn't really working out," she said.

Illegal Options

Not long after she and the children moved here, the 1986 immigration bill imposing sanctions on employers who knowingly hire illegal aliens was passed. It was then that she decided to become a maid. A friend in North Bergen told her that a family in Deal, a half hour from where they now live, needed help. "We went together to the couple," Ms. Vasquez said. "We said we wanted visas. That's the only reason I will do this." The couple, who had two sons in elementary school, agreed.

Ms. Vasquez and her husband saw few other options. They could have divorced each other, married citizens for $2,000 to $3,000 each, then divorced the citizens and married each other again. (He knew of people who were doing it.) Or they could have bought false documents stating they lived in the United States before 1982 so that they could apply for amnesty under the new law. (He knew of people doing that as well.)

"It wasn't the right way," he said. "I didn't want to go through that situation."

They concede they have resorted to a few illegal methods to move forward here. Ms. Vasquez's husband's Social Security card not only helped him get the garage job; he also used it to open bank accounts and apply for credit cards. And Ms. Vasquez bought a New York driver's license, paying a Panamanian official $50 and a Department of Motor Vehicles worker $40 to get it.

Buying a Home

But they have made their money in honest jobs, they say. And they have sacrificed. For the first 18 months of her job, until the family moved from their apartment in Hudson County to Ocean County, Ms. Vasquez lived with her employers and saw the family only on weekends. She spent close to $80 of her $100-a-week cash salary on taxis. Her husband, who worked an overnight shift, had to hire a baby-sitter to care for the children. The eldest began having problems in school. The whole family was miserable.

"I cried every night," Ms. Vasquez said. "I lost 40 pounds. I wanted to go back to Panama."

The family then moved to a beach apartment in Deal, and having saved about $10,000, started looking for a house. And because Ms. Vasquez had a work permit and proof that she was in the process of obtaining a visa, they could apply for a mortgage.

When they bought their $110,000 house in Brick Township in November 1989, it took every penny they could save—their combined income was about $40,000—and a small loan from the employers of Ms. Vasquez's husband.

It took nearly seven years for Ms. Vasquez and the children to receive their visas. The applications, like thousands of other visa applications that flood the Immigration and Naturalization Service each year, became mired in bureaucracy.

Her husband had not applied for a visa with the rest of the family because if his request had been denied, he would have had to leave the country, he said. Ms. Vasquez applied for her husband's visa after she received hers because the family's lawyer advised them that visa applications sponsored by a spouse are usually quickly approved. In April 1993, immigration officials requested a copy of their marriage certificate—a good sign, according to their lawyer. Eventually, they hope to become full United States citizens.

Progress on the Job Front

As much as she loathed it, Ms. Vasquez still worked as a maid. For a while, she kept the job because she thought she had to if her husband was to get a visa. But early in 1993, she found out that that wasn't so.

"The lawyers said I just need to be employed," she said. She applied for a job as a social worker for a nonprofit organization; in June 1993, she found out she got the job.

Ms. Vasquez keeps a file of their children's school records on a kitchen counter, with all their report cards, teacher's notes and awards. When their report cards didn't meet her standards, Ms. Vasquez and her husband canceled their cable television.

"We tell the children keep your first language and then work hard to achieve," she said. "That's the two pieces of advice."

Her husband is researching schools offering business courses for the import-export business he wants to start. He firmly believes he will succeed.

"One of the things that has always prompted me," he said, "is the idea that if someone else could do it, [why] can't you?"

Periodical Bibliography

The following articles have been selected to supplement the diverse views presented in this chapter. Addresses are provided for periodicals not indexed in the *Readers' Guide to Periodical Literature*, the *Alternative Press Index*, or the *Social Sciences Index*.

Joan Biskupic	"Figuring Inalienable Rights for Illegal Immigrants," *Washington Post National Weekly Edition*, November 21–27, 1994. Available from Reprints, 1150 15th St. NW, Washington, DC 20071.
Edward J. Boyer and John Cox	"Migrants Tell of Harrowing Flight from Authorities," *Los Angeles Times*, April 5, 1996. Available from Reprints, Times Mirror Square, Los Angeles, CA 90053.
Grace Chang	"Undocumented Latinas," *Socialist Review*, vol. 23, no. 3, 1994.
Linda Chavez	"Correcting the Hispanic Profile," *Crisis*, February 1995. Available from 1511 K St. NW, Suite 525, Washington, DC 20005.
David Finnigan	"Our Cheap Clothes Are Their Horror Stories," *National Catholic Reporter*, December 29, 1995–January 5, 1996. Available from PO Box 419281, Kansas City, MO 64141.
Luis Gutierrez	"The New Assault on Immigrants," *Social Policy*, Summer 1995.
Susan Martin	"Immigration Reform," *ABA Journal*, November 1994. Available from 750 N. Lake Shore Dr., Chicago, IL 60611.
Tom Morganthau	"Fear of an Immigrant Nation," *Newsweek*, May 8, 1995.
New Unionist	"Immigrant Workers Build America. Corporate Emigrants Tear It Down," July 1994. Available from 621 W. Lake St., Suite 210, Minneapolis, MN 55408.
Revolutionary Worker	"Downpressed in El Norte," March 10, 1996. Available from PO Box 3486, Merchandise Mart, Chicago, IL 60654.
Jeffrey Rosen	"The War on Immigrants: Why the Courts Can't Save Us," *New Republic*, January 30, 1995.
Christopher Scheer	"'Illegals' Made Slaves to Fashion," *Nation*, September 11, 1995.
Linda Thom	"Babies, Welfare, and Crime," *Social Contract*, Summer 1995. Available from 316 ½ E. Mitchell St., Petoskey, MI 49770.

For Further Discussion

Chapter 1

1. Bruce Fein argues that the majority of illegal immigrants are employed and should pay for the health care they receive. The *Revolutionary Worker* maintains that denying free health care services to illegal immigrants will lead to more health problems, primarily among women and children. Based on the viewpoints, do you think undocumented residents should receive free health care? Explain your reasoning.

2. Although Peter H. Schuck and Rogers M. Smith argue that U.S. citizenship should not be automatically granted to the children of illegal immigrants at birth, they contend that illegal-immigrant families should have some rights. Based on the viewpoint, what rights do you believe should be afforded to them? Why?

Chapter 2

1. Michael Huffington writes about the "vast stream" of illegal immigrants entering America. Make a list of the adjectives and verbs that Huffington employs to illustrate the problem of illegal immigration. Is his choice of words effective? Why or why not?

2. Identify the sources of information cited by Donald L. Huddle and Frank Sharry. Which author uses these sources more effectively, in your opinion? Explain, using examples from the viewpoints.

3. Gayle Hanson reports on various cases of health care fraud committed by illegal immigrants. Antonio R. Velasco contends that many illegal immigrants do not receive health care. Which author makes the stronger argument? Explain your answer.

Chapter 3

1. In his viewpoint, Pete Wilson argues that the federal government must reinforce U.S. borders, prevent illegal immigrants from entering the country, and reimburse states for the costs of illegal immigration. Thomas E. Lehman maintains that America should reduce its restrictions on illegal immigration and open its borders to all immigrants as an economic stimulus. Whose argument do you think is more convincing, and why?

2. Bill Clinton advocates increased federal funding to combat illegal immigration. Do you agree that increased spending can reduce the number of illegal immigrants entering America? Why or why not? If yes, rank in order of importance the various ways that funds should be allocated.

3. Gary P. Freeman contends that interest groups have been successful at weakening federal efforts to control immigration. Identify groups that would benefit from the presence of illegal immigrants. How would they benefit, in your opinion?

4. Peter Andreas maintains that a better trained and equipped U.S. Border Patrol may make America's border policy more efficient but not necessarily more effective. How would Laurie E. Ekstrand respond to this view?

Chapter 4

1. In her viewpoint criticizing illegal immigrants and their advocates, Ruth Coffey uses the term "illegal aliens." In your opinion, what negative connotations, if any, does this term evoke? Explain your answer.

2. The *Revolutionary Worker* cites the testimony of an undocumented single mother who spent fifteen years working long hours for low pay as a garment worker. What other options do you think this mother could have chosen to support herself and her children? Explain.

Organizations to Contact

The editors have compiled the following list of organizations concerned with the issues debated in this book. The descriptions are derived from materials provided by the organizations. All have publications or information available for interested readers. The list was compiled on the date of publication of the present volume; names, addresses, phone and fax numbers, and e-mail addresses may change. Be aware that many organizations take several weeks or longer to respond to inquiries, so allow as much time as possible.

American Friends Service Committee (AFSC)
Immigrant and Refugee Rights Project
1501 Cherry St.
Philadelphia, PA 19107
(215) 241-7128
fax: (215) 241-7119

AFSC is a Quaker organization committed to peace, social justice, and humanitarian service. The committee works with immigrants in the United States and abroad at over twenty program sites and monitors abuses of human rights by U.S. Border Patrol agents along the U.S.-Mexico border. Its numerous publications include *Sealing Our Borders: The Human Toll, In Their Presence: Reflections on the Transforming Power of Undocumented Immigrants*, and *Borders and Quaker Values*.

American Immigration Control Foundation (AICF)
PO Box 525
Monterey, VA 24465
(540) 468-2022
fax: (540) 468-2024

AICF is an independent research and education organization that believes massive immigration, especially illegal immigration, is harming America. It calls for an end to illegal immigration and for stricter controls on legal immigration. The foundation publishes the monthly newsletter *Border Watch* and the book *Immigration Out of Control: The Interests Against America*.

Americans for Immigration Control (AIC)
725 Second St. NE, Suite 307
Washington, DC 20002
(202) 543-3719
fax: (202) 543-5811

AIC is a lobbying organization that works to influence Congress to adopt legal reforms that would reduce U.S. immigration. It calls for increased funding for the U.S. Border Patrol and the deployment of military forces to prevent illegal immigration. It also opposes amnesty for illegal immigrants. AIC offers articles and brochures explaining its position on immigration issues and publishes *Immigration Watch* twice a year.

California Coalition for Immigration Reform (CCIR)
PO Box 2744-117
Huntington Beach, CA 92649
(714) 921-7142
fax: (714) 846-9682

CCIR is a grassroots volunteer organization representing Americans concerned with illegal immigration. It seeks to educate and inform the public and to effectively ensure enforcement of the nation's immigration laws. CCIR publishes alerts, bulletins, and the monthly newsletter *911*.

Center for Immigration Studies
1815 H St. NW, Suite 1010
Washington, DC 20006-3604
(202) 466-8185
fax: (202) 466-8076
e-mail: center@cis.org

The center researches and analyzes the social, economic, environmental, and demographic effects of immigration on America. Among its numerous publications on immigration is the quarterly journal *Immigration Review*.

Federation for American Immigration Reform (FAIR)
1666 Connecticut Ave. NW, Suite 400
Washington, DC 20009
(202) 328-7004
fax: (202) 387-3447

FAIR works to stop illegal immigration and to limit legal immigration. It believes that the growing flood of immigrants into the United States causes higher unemployment and drains social services. FAIR publishes the monthly newsletter *FAIR Immigration Report* and the bimonthly *FAIR Information Exchange* as well as many reports and position papers.

League of United Latin American Citizens (LULAC)
221 N. Kansas St., Suite 1200
El Paso, TX 79901
(915) 577-0726
fax: (915) 577-0914

LULAC is an organization of Hispanic Americans concerned with seeking full social, political, economic, and educational rights for Hispanics in the United States. It offers employment training programs and conducts research on postsecondary education and its relation to Hispanic youth. LULAC publishes *HOPE Voter's Guide* and the monthly *LULAC News*.

Mexican American Legal Defense and Educational Fund (MALDEF)
634 S. Spring St., 11th Fl.
Los Angeles, CA 90014
(213) 629-2512
fax: (213) 629-3120

MALDEF is a national organization that promotes and protects the civil rights of Latinos in the United States through educational outreach, advocacy, leadership development training, law school and communications scholarships, and the legal system. It publishes the biannual newsletters *MALDEF* and *Leading Hispanics*.

National Council of La Raza (NCLR)
1111 19th St. NW, Suite 1000
Washington, DC 20036
(202) 785-1670
fax: (202) 776-1794

NCLR is a national organization that seeks to improve opportunities for Americans of Hispanic descent. It conducts research on many issues, including immigration, and opposes restrictive immigration laws. The council publishes and distributes congressional testimonies and reports, including *Unfinished Business: The Immigration Control and Reform Act of 1986, Unlocking the Golden Door: Hispanics and the Citizenship Process*, and the quarterly newsletter *Agenda*.

National Immigration Forum
220 I St. NE, Suite 220
Washington, DC 20002-4362
(202) 544-0004
fax: (202) 544-1905

The forum believes legal immigrants strengthen America and that welfare benefits do not attract illegal immigrants. It supports effective measures aimed at curbing illegal immigration and promotes programs and policies that help refugees and immigrants assimilate into American society. The forum publishes the quarterly newsletter the *Golden Door* and the bimonthly newsletter *Immigration Policy Matters*.

National Network for Immigrant and Refugee Rights
310 Eighth St., Suite 307
Oakland, CA 94607
(510) 465-1984
fax: (510) 465-1885
e-mail: nnirr@igc.apc.org

The network includes community, church, labor, and legal groups committed to the cause of equal rights for all immigrants. These groups work to end discrimination against and unfair treatment of illegal immigrants and refugees. The network aims to strengthen and coordinate educational efforts among immigration advocates nationwide. It publishes a quarterly newsletter, *Network News*.

U.S. Border Patrol
San Diego Sector Public Information Office
PO Box 439022
San Diego, CA 92143-9022
(619) 662-7258
fax: (619) 662-7463

The Border Patrol is the mobile, uniformed enforcement arm of the Immigration and Naturalization Service. The agency's mission is to maintain control of the international boundaries between ports of entry by detecting and preventing the smuggling and unlawful entry of immigrants into the United States. It publishes various brochures, including *Operation Gatekeeper: Landmark Progress at the Border*.

U.S. Commission on Immigration Reform
2430 E St. NW, South Bldg.
Washington, DC 20037
(202) 776-8642

The organization is a bipartisan congressional commission whose final report is due in September 1997. The commission published its first interim report, *U.S. Immigration Policy: Restoring Credibility*, in September 1994 and its second interim report, *Legal Immigration: Setting Priorities*, in June 1995. It also publishes the quarterly newsletter *CIR News*.

Voice of Citizens Together (VCT)
13601 Ventura Blvd., Suite 163
Sherman Oaks, CA 91423
(818) 501-2061
fax: (818) 501-0359
web site: www.instanet.com/~vct

VCT is a grassroots organization that collects and disseminates information on immigration. Its members believe that uncontrolled immigration presents a threat to the community, economy, and culture of the United States. VCT publishes a monthly newsletter that presents its findings on immigration.

Bibliography of Books

Phillip Anastos and *Illegal: Seeking the American Dream.* New York:
Chris French Rizzoli, 1991.

Peter Brimelow *Alien Nation: Common Sense About America's Immigration Disaster.* New York: Random House, 1995.

Leo R. Chavez *Shadowed Lives: Undocumented Immigrants in American Society.* Orlando, FL: Harcourt Brace Jovanovich, 1992.

Wayne A. Cornelius *The Uncertain Connection: Free Trade and Mexico-*
and Philip L. Martin *U.S. Migration.* San Diego: Center for U.S.-Mexican Studies, 1993.

Wayne A. Cornelius *Controlling Immigration.* Stanford, CA: Stanford
et al., eds. University Press, 1994.

Humphrey Dalton, ed. *Will America Drown? Immigration and the Third World Population Explosion.* Washington, DC: Scott Townsend, 1995.

Venson C. Davis *Blood on the Border: Criminal Behavior and Illegal Immigration Along the Southern U.S. Border.* New York: Vantage Press, 1993.

Lisa Duran et al. *Immigrant Rights—and Wrongs.* Los Angeles: Labor/Community Strategy Center, 1994.

Richard M. Ebeling *The Case for Free Trade and Open Immigration.*
and Jacob G. Washington, DC: Future of Freedom Founda-
Hornberger, eds. tion, 1995.

Todd A. Eisenstadt *Caring Capacity Versus Carrying Capacity: Com-*
and Cathryn L. *munity Responses to Mexican Immigration in San*
Thorup *Diego's North County.* San Diego: Center for U.S.-Mexican Studies, 1994.

Jonathan L. Fried *Operation Blockade: A City Divided.* Philadel-phia: American Friends Service Committee, 1994.

General Accounting *Border Control: Revised Strategy Is Showing Some*
Office *Positive Results.* Washington, DC: U.S. Government Printing Office, December 1994.

William R. Hawkins *Importing Revolution: Open Borders and the Radical Agenda.* Monterey, VA: American Immigration Control Foundation, 1995.

David M. Heer

Undocumented Mexicans in the United States. New York: Cambridge University Press, 1990.

Robert E. Holmes

The Criminal Alien. Sacramento, CA: Senate Publications, 1993.

Daniel James

Illegal Immigration: An Unfolding Crisis. Lanham, MD: University Press of America, 1990.

Wayne Lutton and John Tanton

The Immigration Invasion. Petoskey, MI: Social Contract Press, 1994.

Sarah J. Mahler

American Dreaming: Immigrant Life on the Margins. Princeton, NJ: Princeton University Press, 1995.

Nicolaus Mills and Toni Morrison, eds.

Arguing Immigration: The Debate over the Changing Face of America. New York: Simon & Schuster, 1994.

Alexander Monto

The Roots of Mexican Labor Migration. Westport, CT: Praeger, 1994.

Harry Pachon and Louis Desipio

New America by Choice: Political Perspectives of Latino Immigrants. Boulder, CO: Westview, 1994.

Ramón "Tianguis" Pérez

Diary of an Undocumented Immigrant. Translated by Dick J. Reavis. Houston: Arte Publico Press, 1991.

Rockford Institute

Immigration and the American Identity: Selections from Chronicles: A Magazine of American Culture, *1985–1995.* Rockford, IL: Rockford Institute, 1995.

Jeanne Schinto

Huddle Fever: Living in the Immigrant City. New York: Knopf, 1995.

Julian L. Simon

Immigration: The Demographic and Economic Facts. Washington, DC: Cato Institute/National Immigration Forum, 1995.

Robert Suro

Remembering the American Dream: Hispanic Immigration and National Policy. New York: Twentieth Century Fund, 1994.

Sanford J. Ungar

Fresh Blood: The New American Immigrants. New York: Simon & Schuster, 1995.

Philip Q. Yang

Post-1965 Immigration to the United States. Westport, CT: Praeger, 1995.

Index